taste of home
almost homemade

taste of home

Editor-in-Chief: Catherine Cassidy

Vice President, Executive Editor/Books:
Heidi Reuter Lloyd

Creative Director: Howard Greenberg

Food Director: Diane Werner, RD

Senior Editor/Books: Mark Hagen

Editors: Krista Lanphier, Michelle Rozumalski

Associate Creative Director: Edwin Robles Jr.

Art Director: Gretchen Trautman

Content Production Manager: Julie Wagner

Graphic Design Associate: Juli Schnuck

Copy Chief: Deb Warlaumont Mulvey

Copy Editor: Alysse Gear

Recipe Asset System Manager: Coleen Martin

Recipe Testing & Editing: Taste of Home Test Kitchen

Food Photography: Taste of Home Photo Studio

Administrative Assistant: Barb Czysz

North American Chief Marketing Officer:
Lisa Karpinski

Vice President/Book Marketing: Dan Fink

Creative Director/Creative Marketing: Jim Palmen

THE READER'S DIGEST ASSOCIATION, INC.

President and Chief Executive Officer:
Robert E. Guth

ExeUctive Vice President, RDA, and
President, North America:
Dan Lagani

International Standard Book Number (10): 0-89821-985-X
International Standard Book Number (13): 978-0-89821-985-2
Library of Congress Number: 2011936706

COVER PHOTOGRAPHY

Photographer: Rob Hagen

Food Stylist: Kaitlyn Besasie

Set Stylist: Melissa Haberman

PICTURED ON FRONT COVER:
Home-Style Stew, p. 171

PICTURED ON BACK COVER:
Raspberry Butter Torte, p. 149
Sloppy Joe Calzones, p. 136

For other Taste of Home books and products, visit us at
tasteofhome.com

table of contents

Homemade Flavor without the Work!

If some of your days are so busy that it seems nearly impossible to make a wholesome dinner for your family, look no further than Taste of Home Almost Homemade, a wonderful collection of fast, delicious meals and hearty, home-cooked food!

These 288 delicious dishes provide a happy medium between labor-heavy, from-scratch food and packaged or frozen meals. The result? Recipes that are made from convenience products plus a few other ingredients, creating dishes that won't take up loads of time in the kitchen yet still look and taste like they've been made from scratch!

We first had Aunt Dolly's potpie at a family get-together. We loved it and were so happy she shared the recipe. Now, we make it almost every time we bake a ham.

Mary Zinsmeister • Slinger, WI

Easy Shortcuts
with Impressive Results

For busy cooks, it just makes sense to use off-the-shelf ingredients to add a flavor boost to a recipe or to make preparation easier. Dried sauce mixes, jarred chutney, prepared pesto or canned artichoke hearts are efficient ways to jazz up dishes.

While at the supermarket, pick up ready-made items, such as creamy canned soups, frozen puff pastry, biscuit mix or rotisserie chicken, then add a few ingredients for a dish that's faster and tastier than takeout!

These hearty, fast-as-a-flash meals are the perfect solution to your dinnertime duties. You'll find dozens of recipes, from tasty appetizers to luscious desserts, that won't break the bank but will lighten up the task of mealtime preparation. Don't worry—we'll keep these amazing shortcuts a secret. Your family won't be able to tell the difference between these dishes and ones that are completely homemade!

Reliable Recipes from
Home Cooks Just Like You!

Every recipe in this cheery cookbook has been tasted and approved by our Test Kitchen professionals, so you can be sure that you are serving your family the best. Plus, the recipes come from time-crunched cooks just like you! You'll also find helpful tips throughout the book that offer food and cooking advice.

With easy-to-follow directions and beautiful color photographs, Taste of Home Almost Homemade will be the most valuable recipe source in your kitchen!

These yummy, easy–to fix morsels are ready in a jiffy, leaving you plenty of time to spend preparing other recipes or bonding with family and friends.

snacks & appetizers

artichoke bread

PREP: 30 MIN. + COOLING • BAKE: 15 MIN.

1 tube (11 ounces) refrigerated crusty French loaf

1 can (14 ounces) water-packed artichoke hearts, rinsed, drained and chopped

1/2 cup seasoned bread crumbs

1/3 cup grated Parmesan cheese

1/3 cup reduced-fat mayonnaise

2 garlic cloves, minced

1 cup (4 ounces) shredded part-skim mozzarella cheese

1 Bake loaf according to package directions; cool. Cut bread in half lengthwise; place on an ungreased baking sheet.

2 In a small bowl, combine the artichokes, bread crumbs, Parmesan cheese, mayonnaise and garlic; spread evenly over cut sides of bread. Sprinkle with mozzarella cheese.

3 Bake at 350° for 15-20 minutes or until cheese is melted. Slice and serve warm.

YIELD: 1 LOAF (12 SLICES).

chutney-bacon cheese ball

PREP: 30 MIN. + CHILLING

1 package (8 ounces) cream cheese, softened

2 cups (8 ounces) shredded sharp cheddar cheese

1 jar (9 ounces) chutney

1 pound bacon strips, chopped

6 green onions, finely chopped

Assorted crackers

1 In a large bowl, combine cheeses. Shape into a ball; top with chutney. Cover and refrigerate for 8 hours or overnight.

2 In a large skillet, cook bacon over medium heat until crisp. Remove to paper towels; drain. Sprinkle bacon and onions over cheese ball. Serve with crackers.

YIELD: 4-1/2 CUPS.

garlic pizza wedges

PREP/TOTAL TIME: 25 MIN.

Our pastor made this for a get-together, and my husband and I just couldn't stay away from the hors d'oeuvres table. The cheesy slices taste great served warm, but they're still wonderful when they've cooled slightly.

Krysten Johnson • Simi Valley, CA

1 prebaked 12-inch pizza crust

1 cup grated Parmesan cheese

1 cup mayonnaise

1 small red onion, chopped

3-1/2 teaspoons minced garlic

1 tablespoon dried oregano

1 Place the crust on an ungreased 14-in. pizza pan. In a small bowl, combine the Parmesan cheese, mayonnaise, onion, garlic and oregano; spread over crust. Bake at 450° for 8-10 minutes or until edges are lightly browned. Cut into wedges.

YIELD: 2 DOZEN.

tortellini appetizers

PREP: 20 MIN. • BAKE: 20 MIN. + COOLING

4 garlic cloves, peeled

2 tablespoons olive oil, divided

1 package (9 ounces) refrigerated spinach
   tortellini

1 cup mayonnaise

1/4 cup grated Parmesan cheese

1/4 cup milk

1/4 cup prepared pesto

1/8 teaspoon pepper

1 pint grape tomatoes

26 frilled toothpicks

1 Place garlic cloves on a double thickness of heavy-
   duty foil; drizzle with 1 tablespoon oil. Wrap foil
   around garlic. Bake at 425° for 20-25 minutes or
   until tender. Cool for 10-15 minutes.

2 Meanwhile, cook the tortellini according to package
   directions; drain and rinse in cold water. Toss
   with the remaining oil; set aside. In a small bowl,
   combine the mayonnaise, Parmesan cheese, milk,
   pesto and pepper. Mash garlic into pesto mixture;
   stir until combined.

3 Alternately thread the tortellini and tomatoes
   onto toothpicks. Serve with the pesto dip.
   Refrigerate leftovers.

YIELD: ABOUT 2 DOZEN (1-1/2 CUPS DIP).

Mini tart shells are filled with a cream cheese mixture, then topped with seafood sauce and shrimp for this picture-perfect, tasty appetizer. You could also serve several as a fast, light meal.

Gina Hutchison
Smithville, MO

shrimp tartlets

PREP/TOTAL TIME: 15 MIN.

- 1 package (8 ounces) cream cheese, softened
- 1-1/2 teaspoons Worcestershire sauce
- 1 to 2 teaspoons grated onion
- 1 teaspoon garlic salt
- 1/8 teaspoon lemon juice
- 2 packages (1.9 ounces each) frozen miniature phyllo tart shells
- 1/2 cup seafood cocktail sauce
- 30 cooked medium shrimp, peeled and deveined

1 In a small bowl, combine the first five ingredients. Spoon into tart shells. Top with seafood sauce and shrimp. Refrigerate until serving.

YIELD: 2-1/2 DOZEN.

smoked salmon tomato pizza

PREP/TOTAL TIME: 25 MIN.

This quick and easy appetizer comes in handy when you find yourself in a time crunch. My "honey" likes this recipe so much that he can almost eat the entire thing by himself.

Natalie Bremson • Plantation, FL

- 1 prebaked 12-inch thin pizza crust
- 1 cup whipped cream cheese
- 4 ounces smoked salmon or lox, cut into thin strips
- 1 cup chopped tomato
- 1/4 cup chopped red onion
- 2 tablespoons capers, drained
- 2 tablespoons minced fresh parsley
- Pepper to taste

1 Place the crust on an ungreased 12-in. pizza pan. Bake at 450° for 8-10 minutes or until heated through. Spread with cream cheese.

2 Sprinkle with salmon, tomato, onion, capers, parsley and pepper. Cut into slices.

YIELD: 8 SLICES.

This appetizer has been a real hit at church receptions and family events. With shrimp, a little wine, and phyllo, these tiny tarts will "upscale" any party.

Heather Melnick
Macedon, NY

tempting shrimp phyllo tarts

PREP: 15 MIN. + CHILLING • BAKE: 10 MIN.

4 ounces reduced-fat cream cheese

1/4 cup shredded reduced-fat cheddar cheese

3 tablespoons white wine or fat-free milk

1/2 cup chopped cooked peeled shrimp

1/2 teaspoon onion powder

1/2 teaspoon salt

1/4 to 1/2 teaspoon dried thyme

2 packages (1.9 ounces each) frozen miniature phyllo tart shells

1 In a small bowl, combine the cream cheese, cheddar cheese and wine or milk. Stir in the shrimp, onion powder, salt and thyme. Cover and refrigerate for at least 2 hours to allow flavors to blend.

2 Spoon filling by heaping teaspoonfuls into tart shells. Place on an ungreased baking sheet. Bake at 350° for 8-12 minutes or until shells are lightly browned. Serve warm. Refrigerate leftovers.

YIELD: 2-1/2 DOZEN.

crab 'n' brie strudel slices

PREP: 45 MIN. • BAKE: 20 MIN.

Mouthwatering Brie, succulent crab and a hint of pear make this delicate pastry a favorite.

Jennifer Pfaff • Indianapolis, IN

1/2 pound fresh crabmeat

6 ounces Brie cheese, rind removed, cut into 1/4-inch cubes

2-1/2 cups finely chopped peeled ripe pears

1/2 cup thinly sliced green onions

1/2 cup diced fully cooked ham

2 teaspoons lemon juice

1 garlic clove, minced

Dash pepper

14 sheets phyllo dough (14 inches x 9 inches)

3/4 cup butter, melted

1 In a large bowl, combine the first eight ingredients; set aside.

2 Place one sheet of phyllo dough on a work surface; brush with butter. Repeat with 6 more sheets of phyllo, brushing each layer with butter. (Keep remaining phyllo covered with plastic wrap and a damp towel to prevent it from drying out.)

3 Spread half of crab filling to within 1 in. of edges. Fold the two short sides over filling. Starting with the long side, roll up jelly-roll style.

4 Transfer to a greased 15-in. x 10-in. x 1-in. baking pan. Brush top with the butter; score top lightly at 1-in. intervals. Repeat with the remaining phyllo, butter and filling.

5 Bake at 375° for 20-25 minutes or until golden brown. Let stand for 5 minutes. Cut into slices along scored lines.

YIELD: 2 DOZEN.

We fashion festive star treats from convenient frozen puff pastry in this dish. Feel free to experiment with different seasonings.
Taste of Home Test Kitchen

puff pastry stars

PREP/TOTAL TIME: 30 MIN.

1 frozen puff pastry, thawed

2 tablespoons canola oil

1 tablespoon ranch salad dressing mix

3 tablespoons shredded Parmesan cheese

1 Unfold puff pastry. In a small bowl, combine oil and dressing mix; brush over pastry. Using a floured 3-in. star-shaped cookie cutter, cut out 10 stars. Place on a greased baking sheet. Sprinkle with cheese.

2 Bake at 400° for 7-9 minutes or until puffy and golden brown. Serve warm.

YIELD: 10 APPETIZERS.

chutney-topped brie

PREP/TOTAL TIME: 15 MIN.

1 round (8 ounces) Brie cheese
1/4 cup chutney
2 tablespoons real bacon bits
Assorted crackers

1 Place the cheese in an ungreased ovenproof serving dish. Top with chutney and bacon. Bake, uncovered, at 400° for 10-12 minutes or until cheese is softened. Serve with crackers.

YIELD: 8 SERVINGS.

orange fruit dip

PREP: 5 MIN. + CHILLING

I often take a platter of fruit and this dip to picnics, bridal showers and family events. Depending on the season, I'll have strawberries, cantaloupe, apples and other fresh fruits.

Susan Kruspe • Shortsville, NY

1-1/2 cups cold milk
1 can (6 ounces) frozen orange juice concentrate, thawed
1 package (3.4 ounces) instant vanilla pudding mix
1/4 cup sour cream
Assorted fresh fruit

1 In a large bowl, whisk milk, orange juice concentrate and pudding mix for 2 minutes. Let stand for 2 minutes or until soft-set. Whisk in sour cream.

2 Cover and refrigerate for at least 4 hours. Serve with fresh fruit.

YIELD: 2-3/4 CUPS.

pepperoni cheese twists

PREP: 25 MIN. • BAKE: 10 MIN.

3 tablespoons finely chopped oil-packed sun-dried tomatoes plus 1 teaspoon oil from the jar

1/3 cup finely chopped pepperoni

1/3 cup shredded Parmesan cheese

1-1/2 teaspoons minced fresh rosemary or 1/2 teaspoon dried rosemary, crushed

1 teaspoon water

Dash garlic powder

Dash pepper

1 tube (13.8 ounces) refrigerated pizza crust

1 In a small bowl, combine the tomatoes and their oil, pepperoni, cheese, rosemary, water, garlic powder and pepper.

2 On a lightly floured surface, roll dough into a 14-in. x 10-in. rectangle. Spread tomato mixture lengthwise over half of dough. Fold dough over filling; press edges to seal. Cut widthwise into fourteen 1-in.-wide strips. Fold each strip in half; twist two or three times. Place 1 in. apart on a greased baking sheet.

3 Bake at 425° for 6-8 minutes or until golden brown.

YIELD: 14 CHEESE TWISTS.

shredded parm

If you buy a chunk of Parmesan and grate your own, use the finest section on the grating tool. To use a food processor, cut the cheese into 1-inch cubes and process 1 cup of cubes at a time on high until finely grated.

Elegant occasions require fancy appetizers like this. Family and friends will be surprised to hear just how easy it is to prepare.

Gail Cawsey
Sequim, WA

garlic brie pizza

PREP: 10 MIN. • BAKE: 40 MIN.

3 whole garlic bulbs
2 tablespoons olive oil
12 ounces Brie cheese
1 prebaked 12-inch pizza crust
1/2 cup sliced almonds, toasted

1 Remove papery outer skin from garlic (do not peel or separate cloves). Cut the top off each garlic bulb. Brush with oil. Wrap each bulb in heavy-duty foil; place on a baking sheet. Bake at 425° for 30-35 minutes or until softened. Cool for 10-15 minutes. Squeeze softened garlic into a small bowl and mash.

2 Remove rind from Brie and discard. Cut Brie into 1/4-in. slices. Place crust on a 12-in. pizza pan. Spread with garlic. Arrange cheese slices over garlic; sprinkle with almonds. Bake at 450° for 8-10 minutes or until cheese is melted.

YIELD: 10 SERVINGS.

confetti cheese salsa

PREP/TOTAL TIME: 20 MIN.

This creamy cheese dip is so quick and easy that it can be served during any season. It's always a big hit at Fourth of July picnics. I never have to worry about covering the dish on the picnic table because the mixture disappears in no time.

Deidra Engle • Aledo, IL

2 cups (8 ounces) finely shredded cheddar cheese
2 cups (8 ounces) shredded part-skim mozzarella cheese
2 large tomatoes, seeded and chopped
1 medium green pepper, diced
1 small cucumber, seeded and diced
1 small onion, chopped
1 bottle (8 ounces) ranch salad dressing
2 tablespoons salsa
Corn or tortilla chips

1 In a large bowl, combine the first six ingredients. Combine the salad dressing and salsa; pour over cheese mixture and toss gently. Serve with chips. Refrigerate leftovers.

YIELD: 7 CUPS.

hot chicken swirls

PREP: 25 MIN. • BAKE: 10 MIN.

2 tubes (8 ounces each) refrigerated reduced-fat crescent rolls

1 cup shredded cooked chicken breast

4 ounces fat-free cream cheese

1/4 cup reduced-fat ranch salad dressing

1/4 cup shredded reduced-fat cheddar cheese

1/4 cup finely chopped sweet red pepper

2 green onions, finely chopped

2 tablespoons Louisiana-style hot sauce

1 Separate each tube of crescent dough into four rectangles; gently press perforations to seal. In a small bowl, combine the remaining ingredients; spread evenly over rectangles. Roll up jelly-roll style, starting with a short side; pinch seams to seal.

2 Cut each into eight slices; place cut side down on ungreased baking sheets. Bake at 375° for 10-12 minutes or until golden brown. Refrigerate the leftovers.

YIELD: 64 APPETIZERS.

tomato bacon cups

PREP: 20 MIN. • BAKE: 10 MIN./BATCH

I got the recipe for these savory biscuits at a friends house one Thanksgiving. I've made them at special gatherings ever since and they always disappear fast.

Paige English • Saint Helens, OR

1 small tomato, finely chopped

1/2 cup mayonnaise

1/2 cup real bacon bits

1/2 cup shredded Swiss cheese

1 small onion, finely chopped

1 teaspoon dried basil

1 tube (12 ounces) refrigerated buttermilk biscuits, separated into 10 biscuits

1 In a small bowl, combine the tomato, mayonnaise, bacon, cheese, onion and basil; set aside. Split each biscuit into three layers; press each layer into an ungreased miniature muffin cup.

2 Spoon tomato mixture into cups. Bake at 450° for 8-10 minutes or until golden brown. Serve warm.

YIELD: 2-1/2 DOZEN.

shrimp napoleons

PREP: 20 MIN. • BAKE: 15 MIN. + COOLING

Flaky and tender frozen puff pastry serves as the bread for these cold shrimp sandwiches. Bake the pastry and prepare the filling a day ahead, then simply assemble before guests arrive.

Mary Lou Wayman • Salt Lake City, UT

1 package (17.3 ounces) frozen puff pastry, thawed

2 packages (3 ounces each) cream cheese, softened

1 tablespoon thinly sliced green onion

1 tablespoon Dijon mustard

1 teaspoon Worcestershire sauce

2-1/2 cups chopped cooked peeled shrimp

1/3 cup finely shredded carrot

4 bacon strips, cooked and crumbled

1 Line two baking sheets with parchment paper. Unfold one puff pastry sheet on a lightly floured surface. Cut sheet into nine squares, about 3 in. Cut each square in half, forming 18 rectangles.

2 Place on one prepared baking sheet. Repeat with remaining puff pastry. Bake at 425° for 12-15 minutes or until puffed and golden brown. Remove to a wire rack to cool.

3 In a small bowl, beat the cream cheese, onion, mustard and Worcestershire sauce until well blended. Stir in the shrimp, carrot and bacon.

4 To assemble, use a fork to split each pastry in half horizontally. Spread a rounded tablespoonful of cream cheese mixture over the bottom halves; replace tops. Refrigerate until serving.

YIELD: 3 DOZEN.

This chunky and colorful salsa is the ideal companion for crispy tortilla chips. It goes together in a jiffy.

Susan Causey • Columbia, LA

zesty salsa

PREP: 10 MIN. + CHILLING

2 large tomatoes, diced

6 green onions, chopped

1 cup (4 ounces) finely shredded Monterey Jack cheese

1 can (4 ounces) chopped green chilies

1 can (2-1/4 ounces) sliced ripe olives, drained

1/4 cup prepared zesty Italian salad dressing

Tortilla chips

1 In a bowl, combine the first six ingredients; mix well. Cover and refrigerate for at least 1 hour. Serve with tortilla chips.

YIELD: 4 CUPS.

I guarantee you won't be able to stop eating this sweet and savory appetizer once you start. The recipe makes just the right amount for a smaller gathering.

Mimi Merta
Dunedin, FL

pear pizza wedges

PREP/TOTAL TIME: 25 MIN.

2 whole pita breads
2 teaspoons olive oil
1/2 cup crumbled Gorgonzola cheese
1 medium ripe pear, thinly sliced
1/4 cup coarsely chopped walnuts
1 tablespoon honey
1 teaspoon balsamic vinegar

1 Place pita breads on an ungreased baking sheet. Brush with oil; sprinkle with Gorgonzola cheese. Top with pear slices and walnuts.

2 Bake at 400° for 12-15 minutes or until bread is crisp and cheese is melted. Combine the honey and vinegar; drizzle over the pitas. Cut each into four wedges.

YIELD: 8 APPETIZERS.

about vinegar

Balsamic vinegar is made from sweet white grapes and aged in wooden barrels for at least 10 years. You can use cider or mild red wine vinegar instead. White wine vinegar is strong; use sparingly as a substitute.

mozzarella
tomato tartlets

PREP/TOTAL TIME: 20 MIN.

1 garlic clove, minced

1 tablespoon olive oil

1-1/2 cups seeded chopped tomatoes

3/4 cup shredded part-skim mozzarella cheese

1/2 teaspoon dried basil

Pepper to taste

24 frozen miniature phyllo tart shells

6 pitted ripe olives, quartered

Grated Parmesan cheese

1 In a small skillet, saute garlic in oil for 1 minute. Add the tomatoes; cook until liquid has evaporated. Remove from the heat; stir in the mozzarella cheese, basil and pepper.

2 Spoon 1 teaspoonful into each tart shell. Top each with an olive piece; sprinkle with Parmesan cheese. Place on an ungreased baking sheet. Bake at 450° for 5-8 minutes or until bubbly.

YIELD: 2 DOZEN.

taquitos with salsa

PREP/TOTAL TIME: 15 MIN.

2 packages (9 ounces each) frozen steak
 quesadilla rolls

1 jar (16 ounces) lime-garlic salsa

1 can (10 ounces) diced tomatoes and green
 chilies, drained

2 green onions, thinly sliced

2 tablespoons minced fresh parsley

2 tablespoons minced fresh cilantro

2 teaspoons minced garlic

1/2 teaspoon onion salt

1/2 teaspoon pepper

1 Prepare quesadilla rolls according to package
 directions for microwave cooking. Meanwhile, for
 salsa, combine the remaining ingredients in a small
 bowl. Serve with quesadilla rolls.

YIELD: 1 DOZEN (2-1/2 CUPS SALSA).

*We jazzed up store-bought quesadilla rolls
from the grocer's freezer section with a spicy salsa
that's a breeze to stir up. Serve the combo as
an appetizer, snack or quick dinner.*
Taste of Home Test Kitchen

champion chicken puffs

PREP/TOTAL TIME: 30 MIN.

*My guests peeled rubber getting to the table to munch on
these tender bites. They're made with hassle-free refrigerated
crescent rolls and a flavorful chicken and cream cheese filling.*

Amber Kimmich • Powhatan, VA

4 ounces cream cheese, softened

1/2 teaspoon garlic powder

1/2 cup shredded cooked chicken

2 tubes (8 ounces each) refrigerated crescent rolls

1 In a small bowl, beat cream cheese and garlic
 powder until smooth. Stir in chicken.

2 Unroll crescent dough; separate into 16 triangles.
 Cut each triangle in half lengthwise, forming two
 triangles. Place 1 teaspoon of chicken mixture in
 the center of each. Fold short side over filling; press
 sides to seal and roll up.

3 Place 1 in. apart on greased baking sheets. Bake at
 375° for 12-14 minutes or until golden brown.
 Serve warm.

YIELD: 32 APPETIZERS.

fresh herbs

To cut, hold herbs over a small
bowl and make 1/8-in to 1/4-in.
cuts with a kitchen shears. You
can freeze chopped herbs in
freezer containers or bags and
just use the amount you need
directly from the freezer.

chicken
crescent appetizer

PREP/TOTAL TIME: 30 MIN.

1 package (12 ounces) frozen spinach souffle
2 cups cubed cooked chicken
1 can (2.8 ounces) french-fried onions
1/2 cup shredded Parmesan cheese
1 tube (8 ounces) refrigerated crescent rolls

1 Heat spinach souffle according to package
directions. Meanwhile, in a small bowl, combine the
chicken, onions and Parmesan cheese; set aside.

2 Unroll the crescent dough; separate into eight
triangles. Arrange on an ungreased 12-in. round
baking pan or pizza pan, forming a ring with
pointed ends facing the outer edge of pan and
wide ends overlapping.

3 Stir souffle into chicken mixture; spoon over wide
ends of rolls. Fold points over filling and tuck under
wide ends (filling will be visible). Bake at 375° for
11-13 minutes or until golden brown.

YIELD: 8 SERVINGS.

chili cheese dip

PREP/TOTAL TIME: 20 MIN.

1 package (8 ounces) cream cheese, softened
1 can (15 ounces) chili without beans
1/4 cup finely chopped green onions
4 to 8 garlic cloves, minced
1 can (4 ounces) chopped green chilies
1 can (16 ounces) refried beans
1 cup (4 ounces) shredded Mexican cheese blend
Breadsticks

1 In a small bowl, beat cream cheese until smooth. Spread into a greased microwave-safe 1-1/2-qt. dish. Layer with chili, onions, garlic, green chilies and refried beans. Sprinkle with cheese.

2 Microwave, uncovered, on high for 6-8 minutes until cheese is melted and edges are bubbly. Serve warm with breadsticks.

YIELD: 5 CUPS.

veggie tortilla pinwheels

PREP/TOTAL TIME: 25 MIN.

2 packages (8 ounces each) cream cheese, softened

1 envelope ranch salad dressing mix

5 green onions, chopped

1 can (4 ounces) chopped green chilies, drained

1 can (3.8 ounces) sliced ripe olives, drained

1 celery rib, chopped

1/4 cup chopped sweet red pepper

2 to 3 tablespoons real bacon bits

8 flour tortillas (10 inches)

1 In a small bowl, beat cream cheese and dressing mix until blended. Beat in the onions, green chilies, olives, celery, red pepper and bacon. Spread over tortillas. Roll up. Cut each into 1-in. slices. Refrigerate leftovers.

YIELD: ABOUT 5 DOZEN.

bacon-cheese biscuit bites

PREP: 20 MIN. • BAKE: 15 MIN.

4 ounces cream cheese, softened

1 egg

1 tablespoon milk

1/3 cup real bacon bits

1/4 cup shredded Swiss cheese

1 tablespoon dried minced onion

1 large plum tomato, seeded and finely chopped, divided

1 tube (10.2 ounces) large refrigerated flaky biscuits

1 In a small bowl, beat the cream cheese, egg and milk until blended. Stir in the bacon, cheese, onion and half of the tomato; set aside.

2 Cut each biscuit into four pieces; press each piece into a greased miniature muffin cup. Fill with cream cheese mixture; top with remaining tomato.

3 Bake at 375° for 14-16 minutes or until golden brown.

YIELD: 20 APPETIZERS.

As a busy stay-at-home mom, I like great-tasting recipes that are easy and that the kids can help prepare. These savory snacks meet both of those requirements.
Margo Lewis • Lake City, MI

pesto crostini

PREP/TOTAL TIME: 25 MIN.

Look no further when you're searching for an elegant appetizer that's easy to put together. A platter of these crostini will disappear quickly!

Diane Kaplan • Riverdale, NJ

1 loaf (1 pound) French bread, cut into 1-inch slices

2 tablespoons butter, softened

1 tablespoon minced garlic

1 cup prepared pesto

3 small tomatoes, thinly sliced

1/2 pound fresh mozzarella cheese, thinly sliced

1 Place bread slices on an ungreased baking sheet. Combine butter and garlic; spread over bread.

2 Broil 3-4 in. from the heat or until lightly browned. Cool slightly. Spread pesto over butter mixture; top with tomatoes and cheese. Broil 3-5 minutes longer or until cheese is melted.

YIELD: 20 APPETIZERS.

EDITOR'S NOTE: Fresh mozzarella can be found in the deli section of most grocery stores.

pizza fondue

PREP/TOTAL TIME: 25 MIN.

2 cans (10-3/4 ounces each) condensed cheddar
  cheese soup, undiluted

1 can (8 ounces) pizza sauce

1/2 cup milk

1/2 teaspoon dried basil

1/2 teaspoon dried oregano

1/4 teaspoon crushed red pepper flakes

1-1/2 cups (6 ounces) shredded pizza
  cheese blend

1/2 cup chopped pepperoni

Italian bread, cubed and toasted

1 In a large saucepan, combine the first six
  ingredients. Add cheese and pepperoni; cook and
  stir over medium heat until cheese is melted.

2 Transfer to a fondue pot and keep warm. Serve with
  bread cubes.

YIELD: 4 CUPS.

fondue tip

To serve a smooth and delicious
cheese fondue, reduce the heat
to low before stirring the cheese
into hot liquids. Cheese can
curdle easily when overheated.
And keep the heat low while
the cheese melts.

caramelized onion tartlets

PREP: 40 MIN. • BAKE: 15 MIN.

2 tablespoons plus 1/2 cup butter, divided
2 large sweet onions, chopped
1/4 cup sugar
3/4 cup hot water
1 tablespoon beef bouillon granules
1 cup (4 ounces) shredded Swiss cheese
8 sheets phyllo dough (14 inches x 9 inches)

1 In a large skillet, melt 2 tablespoons butter over medium heat. Add onions and sugar. Cook over medium heat for 15-20 minutes or until the onions are golden brown, stirring frequently. Stir in water and bouillon. Bring to a boil. Reduce heat; simmer, uncovered, for 5-7 minutes or until liquid has evaporated. Remove from the heat; stir in cheese.

2 Melt remaining butter. Place one sheet of phyllo dough on a work surface; brush with butter. Brush to distribute evenly. Repeat with a second sheet; brush with butter. Cut into 12 squares. (Keep remaining phyllo covered with plastic wrap and a damp towel to prevent drying.) Repeat three times, making 48 squares.

3 Press one square into a greased miniature muffin cup. Top with another square of phyllo, placing corners off center. Spoon about 1 tablespoon onion mixture into cup. Repeat with remaining phyllo squares and onion mixture. Bake at 375° for 10-15 minutes or until golden brown. Serve warm.

YIELD: 2 DOZEN.

cheddar ham cups

PREP/TOTAL TIME: 30 MIN.

2 cups (8 ounces) finely shredded cheddar cheese

2 packages (2-1/2 ounces each) thinly sliced deli ham, chopped

3/4 cup mayonnaise

1/3 cup real bacon bits

2 to 3 teaspoons Dijon mustard

1 tube (10.2 ounces) large refrigerated flaky biscuits

1 In a large bowl, combine the cheese, ham, mayonnaise, bacon and mustard. Split biscuits into thirds. Press onto the bottom and up the sides of ungreased miniature muffin cups. Fill each with about 1 tablespoon of cheese mixture.

2 Bake at 450° for 9-11 minutes or until golden brown and the cheese is melted. Let stand for 2 minutes before removing from the pans. Serve warm.

YIELD: 2-1/2 DOZEN.

appetizer meatballs

PREP/TOTAL TIME: 30 MIN.

2 cups ketchup

1/2 cup water

1/2 cup white vinegar

1/2 cup honey

2 tablespoons Worcestershire sauce

1 tablespoon dried minced onion

1/4 teaspoon pepper

Dash garlic powder

Dash cayenne pepper

1 package (32 ounces) frozen fully cooked homestyle meatballs

1 In a Dutch oven, combine the first nine ingredients. Bring to a boil. Reduce heat; simmer, uncovered for 15 minutes. Meanwhile, thaw meatballs in microwave according to package directions. Stir into sauce; heat through.

YIELD: ABOUT 6 DOZEN.

I made changes to a barbecue sauce recipe to meet my family's taste. When we needed a quick appetizer for a get-together, I tried the sauce over prepared meatballs, and everyone enjoyed it.
Cheryl Crowson • Sundance, WY

festive crab cakes

PREP/TOTAL TIME: 25 MIN.

I love to stir up excitement at parties with these picture-perfect tarts filled with a pleasant combination of cream cheese, crabmeat and cranberry sauce.

Barbara Nowakowski • North Tonawanda, NY

1/3 cup cream cheese, softened

1/4 cup crabmeat, drained, flaked and cartilage removed

2 tablespoons chopped green onions

1 package (1.9 ounces) frozen miniature phyllo tart shells

1/3 cup whole-berry cranberry sauce

1 In a small bowl, combine the cream cheese, crab and onions until blended. Place the tart shells on an ungreased baking sheet.

2 Fill each shell with 1 tablespoon crab mixture. Top each with 1 teaspoon cranberry sauce. Bake at 375° for 12-15 minutes or until heated through.

YIELD: 15 APPETIZERS.

green onions

If you have washed, dried and chopped more green onions than you need in your recipe, store the leftovers in a covered clean glass jar in the refrigerator. They'll last a couple of weeks this way.

It's easy to make breakfast when you have tasty no-fuss recipes at your fingertips. From pancakes to quiche, there's something for everyone!

breakfast & brunch

deluxe breakfast bake

PREP: 15 MIN. + CHILLING • BAKE: 65 MIN. + STANDING

1 package (6 ounces) onion and garlic salad croutons

2 cups (8 ounces) shredded cheddar cheese

1-1/2 cups cubed fully cooked ham

4 eggs

2-3/4 cups milk, divided

3/4 teaspoon ground mustard

1 can (10-3/4 ounces) condensed cream of mushroom soup, undiluted

1 package (26 ounces) frozen shredded hash brown potatoes, thawed

1/2 teaspoon paprika

1/4 teaspoon pepper

1 Place croutons in a greased 3-qt. baking dish. Sprinkle with cheese and ham. In a large bowl, whisk the eggs, 2-1/4 cups milk and mustard; pour over ham and cheese. Cover and refrigerate overnight.

2 Remove from the refrigerator 30 minutes before baking. Combine soup and remaining 1/2 cup milk until blended; spread over casserole. Top with hash browns; sprinkle with paprika and pepper.

3 Cover and bake at 350° for 30 minutes. Uncover; bake 35-40 minutes longer or until edges are browned. Let stand for 10 minutes before serving.

YIELD: 12 SERVINGS.

I love serving these tender little puffs when I entertain during the holiday season. No one is able to resist them, and I need just four basic ingredients to prepare the simple recipe.

Veronica Johnson
Jefferson City, MO

apple sausage puffs

PREP/TOTAL TIME: 25 MIN.

  1 pound bulk pork sausage
  1 medium apple, finely chopped
  3 ounces cream cheese, softened
  3 tubes (8 ounces each) refrigerated crescent rolls

1 In a large skillet, cook sausage and apple over medium heat until meat is no longer pink; drain. Stir in cream cheese.

2 Unroll one tube of crescent dough; separate into eight triangles. Place 1 tablespoon filling on the long side of each triangle. Roll up starting with a long side; pinch seams to seal.

3 Place point side down 2 in. apart on a greased baking sheet. Repeat with remaining crescent dough and filling. Bake at 375° for 10-12 minutes or until golden brown. Serve warm.

YIELD: 2 DOZEN.

This breakfast treat makes for a great kid-friendly meal. Your kids don't like onions? Simply leave them out. And since most of it is made in the microwave, cleanup is a breeze.

Cheryl Reisen
Ashland, NE

glazed apple and sausage with pancakes

PREP/TOTAL TIME: 20 MIN.

2 packages (7 ounces each) brown-and-serve sausage links

1 teaspoon all-purpose flour

3 tablespoons water

1 large apple, peeled and sliced

1/2 cup chopped onion

3 tablespoons brown sugar

8 pancakes or frozen waffles, warmed

1 Heat sausage according to package directions. Meanwhile, in a 1-1/2-qt. microwave-safe dish, combine flour and water. Add apple and onion. Cover and microwave on high for 3 minutes.

2 Stir in brown sugar. Cover and cook on high for 1-2 minutes or until sugar is dissolved. Cut sausage into bite-size pieces. Add to apple mixture. Serve with pancakes.

YIELD: 4 SERVINGS.

The warm aroma of cinnamon and brown sugar helps wake my family. Convenient toast sticks topped with granola, banana and whipped cream carry them through busy days.

Terri McKitrick
Delafield, WI

cherry-granola french toast sticks

PREP/TOTAL TIME: 20 MIN.

1/4 cup heavy whipping cream

3 tablespoons brown sugar

2 tablespoons butter

1 tablespoon dried cherries

1/4 teaspoon ground cinnamon

1/4 teaspoon vanilla extract

1 package (12.7 ounces) frozen French toast sticks

1 medium banana, sliced

1/4 cup granola without raisins

1 For syrup, in a small saucepan, combine the cream, brown sugar, butter, cherries and cinnamon. Bring to a boil over medium heat, stirring constantly. Cook and stir for 2 minutes. Remove from the heat; stir in vanilla.

2 Prepare French toast sticks according to package directions. Serve with banana, granola and syrup.

YIELD: 4 SERVINGS.

EDITOR'S NOTE: This recipe was tested with Eggo French Toaster Sticks.

asparagus eggs benedict

PREP/TOTAL TIME: 15 MIN.

12 fresh asparagus spears, trimmed and cut in half

1 envelope hollandaise sauce mix

6 eggs

3 English muffins, split and toasted

1/2 cup shredded Swiss cheese

Paprika

1 Place asparagus in a steamer basket. Place in a large saucepan over 1 in. of water; bring to a boil. Cover and steam for 3-4 minutes or until crisp-tender. Set aside.

2 Prepare hollandaise sauce according to package directions. Meanwhile, in a large skillet, bring 2-3 in. water to a boil. Reduce heat; simmer gently. Break cold eggs, one at a time, into a custard cup or saucer. Holding the dish close to the surface of the water, slip the eggs, one at a time, into the water.

3 Cook, uncovered, for 3-5 minutes or until the whites are completely set and the yolks begin to thicken. With a slotted spoon, lift each egg out of the water.

4 To assemble, place 4 pieces of asparagus on each muffin half; top with a poached egg; sprinkle with cheese. Top each with about 3 tablespoons hollandaise sauce; garnish with paprika. Serve immediately.

YIELD: 6 SERVINGS.

pumpkin coffee cake

PREP: 15 MIN. • BAKE: 35 MIN. + COOLING

1 package (16 ounces) pound cake mix
3/4 cup canned pumpkin
6 tablespoons water
2 eggs
2 teaspoons pumpkin pie spice
1 teaspoon baking soda
TOPPING:
1/2 cup chopped walnuts
1/2 cup packed brown sugar
1/4 cup all-purpose flour
3 teaspoons butter, melted

1 In a large bowl, combine the first six ingredients; beat on low speed for 30 seconds. Beat on medium for 2 minutes. Pour half of the pumpkin mixture into a greased 9-in. square baking pan.

2 In a small bowl, combine the topping ingredients; sprinkle half over the batter. Carefully spread with remaining batter. Sprinkle with remaining topping (pan will be full).

3 Bake at 350° for 35-40 minutes or until a toothpick inserted near the center comes out clean. Cool on a wire rack.

YIELD: 9 SERVINGS.

It's tough to resist a second piece of this delightful treat full of comforting flavor. It's a breeze to throw together, because it calls for pound cake mix and canned pumpkin.
Sarah Steele • Moulton, AL

sausage cheese brunch squares

PREP: 30 MIN. • BAKE: 30 MIN.

Here's a cheesy sausage dish that always gives my breakfast crowd a stick-to-the-ribs jump start on Christmas morning.

Pat Stevens • Granbury, TX

1 cup biscuit/baking mix
1/3 cup milk
4 tablespoons mayonnaise, divided
1 pound bulk pork sausage
1 cup chopped onion
1 egg
2 cans (4 ounces each) chopped green chilies
2 cups (8 ounces) shredded cheddar cheese

1 In a small bowl, combine the biscuit mix, milk and 2 tablespoons mayonnaise. Spread into a greased 11-in. x 7-in. baking dish.

2 In a large skillet, cook the sausage and onion over medium heat until meat is no longer pink; drain. Spoon over biscuit mixture. In a large bowl, combine the egg, chilies and remaining mayonnaise; spread over sausage mixture. Sprinkle with cheese.

3 Bake, uncovered, at 350° for 30-35 minutes or until golden brown.

YIELD: 6-8 SERVINGS.

light 'n' crispy waffles

PREP/TOTAL TIME: 20 MIN.

2 cups biscuit/baking mix
2 eggs, lightly beaten
1/2 cup canola oil
1 cup club soda
Fresh fruit and maple syrup

1 In a large bowl, combine the biscuit mix, eggs and oil. Add club soda and stir until smooth.

2 Bake in a preheated waffle iron according to manufacturer's directions until golden brown. Serve with fresh fruit and syrup.

YIELD: 12 WAFFLES.

orange coffee cake ring

PREP/TOTAL TIME: 30 MIN.

With just three ingredients, a packaged sweet roll mix is turned into an elegant treat with toasted coconut and cream cheese.

Tiny Dobbin • Winchester, VA

1 tube (13.9 ounces) orange sweet rolls with icing
1 ounce cream cheese, softened
1/2 cup flaked coconut, toasted

1 Set aside icing from sweet rolls. Arrange rolls in a greased 9-in. round baking pan. Bake at 375° for 18-20 minutes or until golden brown.

2 In a small bowl, combine cream cheese and reserved icing. Spread over warm rolls. Sprinkle with coconut. Serve warm.

YIELD: 8 ROLLS.

polynesian parfaits for two

PREP/TOTAL TIME: 15 MIN.

1 cup (16 ounces) pineapple yogurt
1-1/2 tablespoons sugar
Dash ground nutmeg
1/2 cup granola without raisins
1/2 cup mandarin oranges, drained
1/3 cup unsweetened pineapple tidbits
3 tablespoons fresh raspberries

1 Combine the pineapple yogurt, sugar and nutmeg;
spoon into two dishes. Top with the granola,
mandarin oranges, pineapple tidbits and fresh
raspberries.

YIELD: 2 SERVINGS.

good measure

To measure sour cream or yogurt
into a dry measuring cup, spoon
it into the cup, then level the top
by sweeping a metal spatula or
flat side of a knife across the top
of the cup.

strawberries 'n' cream french toast sticks

PREP/TOTAL TIME: 15 MIN.

- 1 container (16 ounces) frozen sweetened sliced strawberries, thawed
- 1/4 to 1/2 teaspoon ground cinnamon
- 1 teaspoon cornstarch
- 2 teaspoons water
- 1 package (12.7 ounces) frozen French toast sticks
- 2 ounces cream cheese, softened
- 1-1/2 teaspoons brown sugar
- 1 ounce white baking chocolate, melted and cooled

1 In a small saucepan, combine strawberries and cinnamon. Combine cornstarch and water until smooth; stir into berries. Bring to a boil; cook and stir for 2 minutes or until thickened.

2 Prepare French toast sticks according to package directions. Meanwhile, in a small bowl, beat cream cheese and brown sugar until light and fluffy. Stir in white chocolate. Serve berry mixture over French toast; dollop with cream cheese topping.

YIELD: 4 SERVINGS.

EDITOR'S NOTE: This recipe was tested with Eggo French Toaster Sticks.

This is a great recipe for entertaining because it's easy yet extremely impressive. No one will guess it takes only minutes to prepare. The creamy brown sugar and pecan filling between the waffles is delectable!

Jenny Flake
Newport Beach, CA

pecan-stuffed waffles

PREP/TOTAL TIME: 15 MIN.

8 frozen waffles

2 packages (3 ounces each) cream cheese, softened

1/2 cup packed brown sugar

1-1/2 teaspoons ground cinnamon

1 teaspoon vanilla extract

1/2 cup chopped pecans

1 cup maple syrup

Confectioners' sugar

4 fresh strawberries, cut in half

1 Toast waffles according to package directions. In a small bowl, beat the cream cheese, brown sugar, cinnamon and vanilla until smooth. Stir in pecans.

2 Spread over four waffles; top with remaining waffles. Drizzle with syrup. Sprinkle with confectioners' sugar; garnish each with a strawberry.

YIELD: 4 SERVINGS.

caramelized onion broccoli quiche

PREP: 55 MIN. + RISING • BAKE: 50 MIN. + STANDING

This is wonderful for brunch or even for supper when paired with a green salad. The combination of broccoli, sweet onions and feta cheese is truly delicious.

Kim Pettipas • Oromocto, New Brunswick

3 cups sliced sweet onions

1 teaspoon sugar

1/2 teaspoon salt

2 teaspoons olive oil

2 cups frozen shredded hash brown potatoes, thawed

1 tube (11 ounces) refrigerated breadsticks

3 cups frozen chopped broccoli, thawed and drained

1 cup (4 ounces) crumbled feta cheese

2 eggs

2 egg whites

3/4 cup fat-free milk

1 In a large nonstick skillet, cook the onions, sugar and salt in oil over low heat for 40 minutes or until onions are softened and liquid has evaporated. Reduce heat to medium-low; add hash browns. Cook 8-10 minutes longer or until potatoes are golden brown. Remove from the heat and set aside.

2 To make crust, unroll breadstick dough onto a lightly floured surface and separate into strips. Pinch several breadsticks together, end to end, forming a rope. Holding one end of rope, loosely coil dough to form a circle. Add remaining breadsticks to coil, one at a time, pinching ends together. Tuck end under; pinch to seal. Cover and let rest for 10 minutes.

3 Roll into a 10-1/2-in. to 11-in. circle. Transfer to an ungreased 9-in. pie plate. Spoon onion mixture into crust. Top with broccoli and cheese.

4 In a large bowl, whisk the eggs, egg whites and milk; pour over cheese (pie plate will be full). Bake 350° for 40 minutes. Cover edges with foil. Bake 10-12 minutes longer or until a knife inserted near the center comes out clean. Let stand for 10 minutes before cutting.

YIELD: 6 SERVINGS.

I need only four ingredients to make these quick and easy sandwiches. My husband likes it when I add a slice of ham between the waffles.
Sonia Daily • Warren, MI

apple waffle grills

PREP/TOTAL TIME: 15 MIN.

4 teaspoons butter

4 frozen waffles, thawed

4 slices process American cheese

1 medium tart apple, thinly sliced

1 In a large skillet, melt butter over medium heat. Add two waffles; top each with one cheese slice, apple slices, and remaining cheese and waffles. Cook until waffles are lightly toasted on both sides and cheese is melted.

YIELD: 2 SERVINGS.

Just four ingredients are all you'll need for this sure-to-be-popular treat. Friends and family will never guess that refrigerated buttermilk biscuits are the base for these golden, jelly-filled doughnuts.

Ginny Watson
Broken Arrow, OK

berry-filled doughnuts

PREP/TOTAL TIME: 25 MIN.

  4 cups canola oil

  1 tube (7-1/2 ounces) refrigerated buttermilk biscuits, separated into 10 biscuits

  3/4 cup seedless strawberry jam

  1 cup confectioners' sugar

1 In an electric skillet or deep-fat fryer, heat oil to 375°. Fry biscuits, a few at a time, for 1-2 minutes on each side or until golden brown. Drain on paper towels.

2 Cut a small hole in the corner of a pastry or plastic bag; insert a very small tip. Fill bag with jam. Push the tip through the side of each doughnut to fill with jam. Dust with confectioners' sugar while warm. Serve immediately.

YIELD: 10 SERVINGS.

frying tip

If you don't have a deep-fat fryer or an electric fry pan with a thermostat, you can use a kettle or Dutch oven together with a thermometer so you can accurately regulate the temperature of the oil.

california quiche

PREP: 15 MIN. • BAKE: 30 MIN.

5 eggs

3/4 cup milk

1/4 teaspoon pepper

4 ounces Havarti cheese, shredded

1 package (3 ounces) cream cheese, cubed

3/4 cup frozen California-blend vegetables, thawed and patted dry

1 medium plum tomato, thinly sliced

1/3 cup butter, softened

1 teaspoon minced garlic

12 slices French bread (1 inch thick)

1 In a small bowl, whisk the eggs, milk and pepper until blended. Stir in cheeses and vegetables.

2 Pour into a greased 9-in. pie plate. Top with tomato slices. Bake at 375° for 30-35 minutes or until a knife inserted near the center comes out clean. Let stand for 5 minutes.

3 Meanwhile, in a small bowl, combine butter and garlic; spread over both sides of each slice of bread. Broil 3-4 in. from the heat for 1-2 minutes on each side or until lightly browned. Serve with quiche.

YIELD: 6 SERVINGS.

brunch pockets

PREP: 25 MIN. • **BAKE: 25 MIN.**

1 package (15 ounces) refrigerated pie crust

2 pineapple slices, cut in half

4 thin slices deli ham

4 thin slices deli turkey

4 slices Swiss cheese

1 egg, lightly beaten

1 Cut each pastry sheet into four wedges. Pat pineapple slices dry with paper towels. Top four pastry wedges with one slice each of ham, turkey, cheese and pineapple, folding meat and cheese to fit if necessary. Top each with a pastry wedge; seal and crimp edges with a fork. Cut slits in pastry.

2 Place on an ungreased baking sheet. Brush lightly with egg. Bake at 350° for 25-30 minutes or until golden brown. Serve warm.

YIELD: 4 SERVINGS.

These hefty handfuls promise a good, hot breakfast with little fuss. Everyone loves the toasty grab-and-go pockets stuffed with pineapple, ham, turkey and cheese.

Jean Kimm
Coeur d' Alene, ID

pecan pancake pizza

PREP/TOTAL TIME: 15 MIN.

Want to feed your family without flipping griddle after griddle of flapjacks? Try this big pancake pizza that bakes in the oven in minutes. Topped with granola and nuts, the wedges are terrific served with syrup.

Taste of Home Test Kitchen

2 cups pancake mix

2 eggs, lightly beaten

1-3/4 cups milk

2 tablespoons canola oil

1 teaspoon maple flavoring

3/4 cup granola cereal without raisins

3/4 cup pecan halves

Maple syrup, optional

1 Place pancake mix in a bowl. Combine the eggs, milk, oil and maple flavoring; add to pancake mix and mix well. Pour into a greased 14-in. pizza pan; sprinkle with granola and pecans.

2 Bake at 425° for 10-12 minutes or until a toothpick inserted near the center comes out clean. Cut into wedges. Serve with syrup if desired.

YIELD: 6-8 SERVINGS.

overnight egg casserole

PREP: 10 MIN. + CHILLING • BAKE: 1 HOUR + STANDING

4 cups frozen shredded hash brown potatoes,
 thawed

1 cup cubed fully cooked ham

1 can (4 ounces) chopped green chilies

1/2 cup shredded Monterey Jack cheese

1/2 cup shredded cheddar cheese

6 eggs

1 can (12 ounces) evaporated milk

1/4 teaspoon pepper

Salsa, optional

1 In a greased 8-in. square baking dish, layer the hash browns, ham, chilies and cheeses. In a large bowl, whisk the eggs, milk and pepper; pour over the casserole. Cover and refrigerate overnight.

2 Remove from the refrigerator 30 minutes before baking. Bake, uncovered, at 350° for 1 hour or until a knife inserted near center comes out clean. Let stand for 5-10 minutes. Serve with salsa if desired.

YIELD: 9 SERVINGS.

brunch pizza

PREP/TOTAL TIME: 20 MIN.

1 prebaked 12-inch pizza crust
1 tablespoon butter
5 eggs, lightly beaten
1 can (14-1/2 ounces) country-style cream gravy
2 cups (8 ounces) shredded cheddar cheese
1/2 cup real bacon bits
1/4 cup cooked pork sausage

1 Place the crust on an ungreased pizza pan or baking sheet. Bake at 425° for 5 minutes. In a large skillet, melt butter over medium heat. Add eggs; cook until soft-set, stirring occasionally.

2 Spread gravy over crust; top with scrambled eggs, cheese, bacon and sausage. Broil 4-6 in. from the heat for 6 minutes or until cheese is melted.

YIELD: 6 SERVINGS.

This brunch recipe is unbelievably quick and easy but also very delicious. It goes well with a bowl of fruit salad.
Angela Hart • Cool Ridge, WV

egg 'n' pepperoni bundles

PREP: 20 MIN. • BAKE: 15 MIN.

My family calls these "one more gift to open" because they are the last present they unwrap on Christmas morning. Everyone's mouths water when they bite into these delicious bundles loaded with great ingredients.

Helen Meadows • Trout Creek, MT

7 sheets phyllo dough (14 inches x 9 inches)
1/2 cup butter, melted
8 teaspoons dry bread crumbs
2 ounces cream cheese, cut into 8 cubes
4 eggs
24 slices pepperoni, quartered or 1-1/2 ounces Canadian bacon, diced
1/3 cup provolone cheese
2 teaspoons minced chives

1 Place one sheet of phyllo dough on a work surface; brush with butter. Top with another sheet of phyllo; brush with butter. Repeat five times. Cut phyllo in half widthwise, then cut in half lengthwise.

2 Carefully place one stack in each of four greased jumbo muffin cups. Brush edges of dough with butter. Sprinkle 2 teaspoons of bread crumbs onto the bottom of each cup. Top each with two cubes of cream cheese.

3 Break each egg separately into a custard cup; gently pour egg over cream cheese. Sprinkle with pepperoni, provolone cheese and chives. Pinch corners of phyllo together to seal. Bake at 400° for 13-17 minutes or until golden brown. Serve warm.

YIELD: 4 SERVINGS.

chile rellenos quiche

PREP: 25 MIN. • BAKE: 35 MIN.

Pastry for single-crust pie (9 inches)

2 tablespoons cornmeal

1-1/2 cups (6 ounces) shredded
    Monterey Jack cheese

1 cup (4 ounces) shredded cheddar cheese

1 can (4 ounces) chopped green chilies

3 eggs

3/4 cup sour cream

1 tablespoon minced fresh cilantro

2 to 4 drops hot pepper sauce, optional

1 Line unpricked pastry shell with a double thickness of heavy-duty foil. Bake at 450° for 8 minutes. Remove foil; bake 5 minutes longer. Cool on a wire rack. Reduce heat to 350°.

2 Sprinkle cornmeal over bottom of pastry shell. In a small bowl, combine cheeses; set aside 1/2 cup for topping. Add chilies to remaining cheese mixture; sprinkle over crust.

3 In a small bowl, whisk the eggs, sour cream, cilantro and hot pepper sauce if desired. Pour into crust; sprinkle with reserved cheese mixture.

4 Bake for 35-40 minutes or until a knife inserted near the center comes out clean. Let stand for 5 minutes before cutting.

YIELD: 6 SERVINGS.

so-easy cheese danish

PREP: 20 MIN. • BAKE: 25 MIN.

A brunch menu just isn't the same without this tender, flaky Danish. The warm cream cheese center is a delightful surprise. Convenient refrigerated crescent roll dough means I can make it in a snap.

Cathleen Bushman • Geneva, IL

2 packages (8 ounces each) cream cheese, softened
1 cup sugar
1 egg yolk
1 teaspoon vanilla extract
2 tubes (8 ounces each) refrigerated crescent rolls
1 egg white, lightly beaten
TOPPING:
1/2 cup sugar
1/2 cup chopped pecans
1/4 teaspoon ground cinnamon

1 In a large bowl, beat cream cheese and sugar until fluffy. Add egg yolk and vanilla; beat on low speed until blended.

2 Unroll one tube of crescent roll dough into one long rectangle; seal seams and perforations. Press onto the bottom of an ungreased 13-in. x 9-in. baking dish. Spread with cream cheese mixture. On a lightly floured surface, press or roll out remaining dough into a 13-in. x 9-in. rectangle. Place over filling; brush with egg white.

3 In a small bowl, combine the sugar, pecans and cinnamon; sprinkle over top. Bake at 350° for 25-30 minutes or until golden brown. Cool slightly on a wire rack; serve warm. Refrigerate leftovers.

YIELD: 15 SERVINGS.

separating eggs

Place an egg separator over a custard cup and crack egg into the separator. As each egg is separated, place yolk in another bowl and empty egg white into a mixing bowl. It's easier to separate eggs when they are cold.

It took mere minutes for our Test Kitchen to toss together these parfaits. The crunchy granola and cashews contrast nicely with the mandarin oranges and yogurt.

Taste of Home Test Kitchen

orange crunch yogurt

PREP/TOTAL TIME: 10 MIN.

1/3 cup granola cereal without raisins
1/3 cup flaked coconut
1/3 cup chopped cashews
3 containers (8 ounces each) orange yogurt
1 can (11 ounces) mandarin oranges, drained

1 In a bowl, combine the granola, coconut and cashews. In each of four parfait glasses or bowls, layer half of a container of yogurt, 2 tablespoons granola mixture, 5 or 6 orange segments, remaining yogurt and remaining granola mixture.

2 Garnish with remaining oranges. Serve immediately.

YIELD: 4 SERVINGS.

bacon & egg burritos

PREP/TOTAL TIME: 25 MIN.

6 bacon strips, diced
1 cup frozen cubed hash brown potatoes
2 tablespoons chopped onion
6 eggs
1/4 cup sour cream
3/4 cup shredded cheddar cheese, divided
2 tablespoons taco sauce
1/2 to 1 teaspoon hot pepper sauce
4 flour tortillas (10 inches), warmed
Sour cream and chopped tomatoes, optional

1 In a large skillet, cook bacon over medium heat until crisp. Using a slotted spoon, remove to paper towels; drain, reserving 1 tablespoon drippings. Saute potatoes and onions in drippings until potatoes are golden brown, stirring occasionally.

2 In a large bowl, whisk eggs and sour cream. Stir in 1/4 cup cheese, taco sauce and hot pepper sauce. Pour over potato mixture; add bacon. Cook and stir over medium heat until eggs are completely set.

3 Spoon about 3/4 cup down the center of each tortilla; sprinkle with remaining cheese. Fold bottom and sides of tortilla over filling. Serve immediately with sour cream and tomatoes if desired.

YIELD: 4 SERVINGS.

This eye-opener features buttermilk biscuits. If you don't have Canadian bacon, try it with turkey bacon or ham.

Nicki Woods
Springfield, MO

special brunch bake

PREP: 10 MIN. • BAKE: 30 MIN.

2 tubes (4 ounces each) refrigerated buttermilk biscuits

3 cartons (8 ounces each) egg substitute

7 ounces Canadian bacon, chopped

1 cup (4 ounces) shredded reduced-fat cheddar cheese

1 cup (4 ounces) shredded part-skim mozzarella cheese

1/2 cup chopped fresh mushrooms

1/2 cup finely chopped onion

1/4 teaspoon pepper

1 Arrange biscuits in a 13-in. x 9-in. baking dish coated with cooking spray. In a large bowl, combine the remaining ingredients; pour over biscuits.

2 Bake, uncovered, at 350° for 30-35 minutes or until a knife inserted near the center comes out clean.

YIELD: 12 SERVINGS.

eggs

You can substitute 2 fresh eggs for every 1/2 cup egg substitute in the recipe. There may be a slight change in texture. Some folks who watch their cholesterol use egg substitute, which mostly contains egg whites.

This chapter is full of supper sidekicks with loads of flavor. You'll find recipes for potato casseroles, veggie bakes, stuffings and much more!

standout side dishes

My easy recipe uses only 6 ingredients. Serve this Asian-flavored side dish with teriyaki-marinated pork tenderloin or chicken.

Carolyn Schmeling
Brookfield, WI

sweet-and-sour zucchini

PREP/TOTAL TIME: 15 MIN.

2 large zucchini, cut into 1/4-inch slices
1-1/2 teaspoons minced fresh gingerroot
2 teaspoons canola oil
1 garlic clove, minced
1/4 cup sweet-and-sour sauce
1/4 teaspoon salt

1 In a large skillet, saute the zucchini and minced ginger in oil for 5 minutes or until the zucchini is crisp-tender. Add the minced garlic; cook 1 minute longer. Stir in the sweet-and-sour sauce and salt; heat through.

YIELD: 4 SERVINGS.

spanish rice

PREP/TOTAL TIME: 30 MIN.

This rice recipe has been in our family for years. It's handy when you're in a hurry for a side dish to complement almost any main dish, not just Tex-Mex fare.

Sharon Donat • Kalispell, MT

1 can (14-1/2 ounces) vegetable broth
1 can (14-1/2 ounces) stewed tomatoes
1 cup uncooked long grain rice
1 teaspoon olive oil
1 teaspoon chili powder
1/4 teaspoon dried oregano
1/4 teaspoon garlic salt

1 In a large saucepan, combine all ingredients. Bring to a boil. Reduce the heat; cover and simmer for 20-25 minutes or until the rice is tender and the liquid is absorbed.

YIELD: 6 SERVINGS.

bacon-cheddar stuffed potatoes

PREP: 25 MIN. • COOK: 25 MIN.

4 medium baking potatoes

1/3 cup mayonnaise

3/4 cup plus 6 tablespoons shredded cheddar cheese, divided

3/4 cup French onion dip

1/2 cup real bacon bits

4 green onions, chopped

1/4 to 1/2 teaspoon pepper

1 Scrub and pierce potatoes; place on a microwave-safe plate. Microwave, uncovered, on high for 18-22 minutes or until tender, turning once. Let stand for 5 minutes or until cool enough to handle.

2 Meanwhile, in a small bowl, combine the mayonnaise, 3/4 cup cheese, dip, bacon bits, green onions and pepper. Cut a thin slice off the top of each potato and discard. Scoop out the pulp, leaving a thin shell. Add pulp to the mayonnaise mixture and mash.

3 Spoon into potato shells. Return to the microwave-safe plate. Sprinkle with remaining cheese. Microwave, uncovered, on high for 5 minutes or until heated through.

YIELD: 4 SERVINGS.

potato bacon casserole

PREP: 20 MIN. • BAKE: 35 MIN.

4 cups frozen shredded hash brown potatoes, thawed

1/2 cup finely chopped onion

8 bacon strips, cooked and crumbled

1 cup (4 ounces) shredded cheddar cheese

1 egg

1 can (12 ounces) evaporated milk

1/2 teaspoon seasoned salt

1 In a greased 8-in. square baking dish, layer half of the hash brown potatoes, onion, bacon and cheese. Repeat layers.

2 In a small bowl, whisk the egg, milk and seasoned salt; pour over potato mixture. Cover and bake at 350° for 30 minutes. Uncover; bake 5-10 minutes longer or until heated through.

YIELD: 8 SERVINGS.

Common fruit and veggies give store-bought stuffing mix flavor that's anything but ordinary. It's an easy alternative to from-scratch stuffing that can take over an hour to make.

Terri McKitrick
Delafield, WI

apple stuffing

PREP/TOTAL TIME: 15 MIN.

1 medium tart apple, chopped
1/2 cup chopped onion
1/4 cup chopped celery
1 tablespoon butter
1 package (6 ounces) stuffing mix

1 In a large skillet, saute the apple, onion and celery in butter until tender. Prepare stuffing mix according to the package directions. Stir in the apple mixture.

YIELD: 5 SERVINGS.

pesto corn

PREP/TOTAL TIME: 10 MIN.

This great side is one of my very favorite comfort foods. The bright flavors of pesto bring out the natural sweetness of corn in this clever combination.

Laurie Bock • Lynden, WA

1 package (16 ounces) frozen corn, thawed
3/4 cup shredded sharp cheddar cheese
1 tablespoon prepared pesto

1 In a small microwave-safe dish, combine all ingredients. Cover and cook on high for 2-3 minutes or until heated through.

YIELD: 3 SERVINGS.

This recipe came about as an experiment. I wanted to make a squash casserole but didn't have crackers, so I substituted instant stuffing mix. My family loved it. It's a good side dish that doubles easily when friends come to visit.

Dot Morgan
McMinnville, TN

stuffing
squash casserole

PREP/TOTAL TIME: 30 MIN.

1-1/2 cups instant stuffing mix

3/4 cup boiling water

1 tablespoon butter

1 medium yellow summer squash, diced, cooked and drained

1 egg, lightly beaten

2 tablespoons grated Parmesan cheese

1 In a large bowl, combine the stuffing mix, water and butter. Let stand for 5 minutes. Add squash and egg.

2 Transfer to greased 1-qt. baking dish; sprinkle with Parmesan cheese. Bake, uncovered, at 350° for 20-25 minutes or until golden brown.

YIELD: 2 SERVINGS.

salsa pasta 'n' beans

PREP/TOTAL TIME: 25 MIN.

8 ounces uncooked bow tie pasta
1/2 cup chopped onion
1 medium sweet yellow pepper, chopped
1 tablespoon olive oil
2 teaspoons minced garlic
1 can (16 ounces) red beans, rinsed and drained
3/4 cup vegetable broth
3/4 cup salsa
2 teaspoons ground cumin
1/3 cup minced fresh cilantro

1 Cook pasta according to package directions.
Meanwhile, in a large skillet, saute onion and yellow
pepper in oil for 3-4 minutes or until crisp-tender.
Add garlic; cook 1-2 minutes longer or until tender.

2 Stir in the beans, broth, salsa and cumin. Bring to
a boil. Reduce heat; simmer, uncovered, for 5-6
minutes or until heated through. Drain pasta; stir
into bean mixture. Sprinkle with cilantro.

YIELD: 4 SERVINGS.

Seasoned with cumin, cilantro and salsa, zesty
noodles and beans add a little zip to dinnertime. For
those who like even more spice, it's easy to change
the salsa to a medium or hot variety.

Laura Lunardi • West Chester, PA

triple-cheese broccoli puff

PREP: 15 MIN. • BAKE: 50 MIN. + STANDING

This rich-tasting side is a must for our Christmas morning menu.
Like any puffy souffle, it will settle a bit after you remove the dish
from the oven, but the pretty golden top is very attractive. I often
toss in some cubed ham for a main course!

Maryellen Hays • Wolcottville, IN

1 cup sliced fresh mushrooms
1 tablespoon butter
1 package (3 ounces) cream cheese, softened
6 eggs
1 cup milk
3/4 cup biscuit/baking mix
3 cups frozen chopped broccoli, thawed
2 cups (8 ounces) shredded Monterey
Jack cheese
1 cup (8 ounces) 4% cottage cheese
1/4 teaspoon salt

1 In a small skillet, saute mushrooms in butter until
tender; set aside. In a large bowl, beat cream
cheese, eggs, milk and biscuit mix just until
combined. Stir in the broccoli, cheeses, salt
and mushrooms.

2 Pour into a greased round 2-1/2-qt. baking dish.
Bake, uncovered, at 350° for 50-60 minutes or until
a thermometer reads 160°. Let stand for 10 minutes
before serving.

YIELD: 6-8 SERVINGS.

veggie cheese casserole

PREP: 10 MIN. • BAKE: 35 MIN.

3 cups frozen chopped broccoli, thawed and drained

1/2 cup biscuit/baking mix

1 cup (8 ounces) sour cream

1 cup (8 ounces) 4% cottage cheese

2 eggs

1/4 cup butter, melted

1/4 teaspoon salt

1 large tomato, thinly sliced and halved

1/4 cup grated Parmesan cheese

1 Arrange the broccoli in a greased 8-in. square baking dish; set aside.

2 In a large bowl, beat the biscuit mix, sour cream, cottage cheese, eggs, butter and salt; pour over broccoli. Arrange tomato slices over the top; sprinkle with Parmesan cheese.

3 Bake, uncovered, at 350° for 35-40 minutes or until a thermometer reads 160°. Let stand for 5 minutes before cutting.

YIELD: 9 SERVINGS.

quick 'n' easy bean pot

PREP: 10 MIN. • BAKE: 1 HOUR

4 bacon strips, diced
1 medium onion, chopped
2 cans (15-3/4 ounces each) pork and beans
2 tablespoons packed brown sugar
2 teaspoons ground mustard
1 teaspoon instant coffee

1 In a large skillet, cook the bacon and onion over medium heat until bacon is crisp; drain. Stir in the beans, brown sugar, mustard and coffee. Pour into an ungreased 1-1/2-qt. baking dish. Cover and bake at 350° for 30 minutes. Uncover and bake 30 minutes longer.

YIELD: 6-8 SERVINGS.

mustard

Ground mustard, also referred to as dry mustard, is made from mustard seeds that have been finely ground. When a recipe calls for prepared mustard, use yellow or brown mustard that is served as a condiment.

lemony herbed rice

PREP/TOTAL TIME: 25 MIN.

3 cups reduced-sodium chicken broth or vegetable broth

1-1/3 cups uncooked long grain rice

1 can (4 ounces) chopped green chilies, drained

3/4 teaspoon salt

1 tablespoon each minced fresh parsley, cilantro and chives

1/2 teaspoon grated lemon peel

1/4 teaspoon pepper

1 In a large saucepan, combine broth, rice, chilies and salt; bring to a boil. Reduce heat; cover and simmer for 15-20 minutes or until rice is tender. Remove from the heat; let stand for 5 minutes. Fluff with a fork and stir in the remaining ingredients.

YIELD: 7 SERVINGS.

pepperoni pasta salad

PREP/TOTAL TIME: 30 MIN.

Bottled Italian dressing and pepperoni add zip to this colorful combination. Serve it right away or assemble it ahead of time. The longer this salad chills the better.

Shannon Lommen • Kaysville, UT

2 cups uncooked tricolor spiral pasta

1 cup cubed cheddar cheese

1 cup coarsely chopped cucumber

1 small tomato, chopped

2 green onions, chopped

28 pepperoni slices

1/2 cup zesty Italian salad dressing

1 Cook pasta according to package directions; drain and rinse in cold water. In a large bowl, combine the pasta, cheese, cucumber, tomato, onions and pepperoni. Add salad dressing and toss to coat. Cover and refrigerate until serving.

YIELD: 4-6 SERVINGS.

golden baked onions

PREP: 20 MIN. • BAKE: 25 MIN.

6 large sweet onions, thinly sliced

1/4 cup butter, cubed

1 can (10-3/4 ounces) condensed cream of
  chicken soup, undiluted

1/2 cup milk

1/8 teaspoon pepper

3 cups (12 ounces) shredded Swiss cheese,
  divided

6 slices French bread (3/4 inch thick)

2 tablespoons butter, melted

1 In a large skillet, saute onions in butter until tender.
  In a large bowl, combine the soup, milk, pepper and
  2 cups cheese. Stir in onions.

2 Transfer to a greased 2-qt. baking dish. Sprinkle
  with remaining cheese. Brush bread slices with
  melted butter on one side. Arrange buttered side
  up over cheese.

3 Bake, uncovered, at 350° for 25-30 minutes or
  until bubbly. If desired, broil 4-6 in. from heat until
  bread is golden brown. Let stand for 5 minutes
  before serving.

YIELD: 6-8 SERVINGS.

1. In a small saucepan, saute celery in butter until tender; set aside. In a large bowl, combine the stuffing cubes, cranberries, pears, pecans, parsley, poultry seasoning and pepper. Add the broth, egg substitute and celery mixture; toss until combined.

2. Spoon into a greased 2-1/2-qt. baking dish. Cover and bake at 325° for 50-60 minutes or until a thermometer inserted near the center reads 160°.

YIELD: 8-10 SERVINGS.

rich mushroom bake

PREP: 20 MIN. • BAKE: 30 MIN.

I developed this dish to camouflage mushrooms from my family. The stuffing gives great flavor, and Parmesan adds the "mandatory" cheese topping for the kids.

Phylis Dillon • Gibsonia, PA

1 pound sliced fresh mushrooms
6 tablespoons butter, divided
2 tablespoons all-purpose flour
1/2 cup milk
1/2 cup beef broth
1/8 teaspoon pepper
1/2 cup crushed seasoned stuffing
1/2 cup grated Parmesan cheese

1. In a large skillet, saute mushrooms in 2 tablespoons butter; remove and set aside. In the same skillet, melt remaining butter; stir in flour until smooth. Gradually add the milk, broth and pepper. Bring to a boil; cook and stir for 2 minutes or until thickened. Return the mushrooms to the pan; stir in stuffing until blended.

2. Transfer to a greased 1-qt. baking dish; sprinkle with Parmesan cheese. Bake, uncovered, at 350° for 30-35 minutes or until bubbly.

YIELD: 6 SERVINGS.

Our family came up with this recipe when we decided to add something new to our traditional Thanksgiving menu. Now the tasty dressing has become a standard dish on our holiday table.

Juanita Haugen • Pleasanton, CA

cranberry pear stuffing

PREP: 15 MIN. • BAKE: 50 MIN.

1 cup chopped celery
1/2 cup butter
1 package (16 ounces) seasoned stuffing cubes
1-1/2 cups dried cranberries
1-1/2 cups chopped ripe pears
1 cup chopped pecans
1/4 cup minced fresh parsley
2 to 3 teaspoons poultry seasoning
1/2 teaspoon pepper
2 cups chicken broth
3/4 cup egg substitute

I have accumulated some delicious recipes that serve large numbers, like my colorful and delicious pasta salad. The flavors blend so well, and there's plenty of creamy dressing.

Marlene Muckenhirn
Delano, MN

creamy italian spiral salad

PREP: 30 MIN. + CHILLING

- 2 packages (16 ounces each) multicolored spiral pasta
- 1 medium bunch broccoli, cut into florets
- 1 medium head cauliflower, cut into florets
- 2 cups frozen peas and carrots
- 2 cups cherry tomatoes, quartered
- 1 cup shredded Parmesan cheese
- 6 green onions, chopped
- 1/2 cup chopped green pepper
- 1 can (2-1/4 ounces) sliced ripe olives, drained
- 2 bottles (16 ounces each) creamy Italian salad dressing

1 Cook pasta according to package directions; drain and rinse in cold water.

2 In a large bowl, combine the pasta, broccoli, cauliflower, peas and carrots, tomatoes, cheese, onions, green pepper and olives. Add the dressing; mix well. Cover and refrigerate for 2-3 hours or until chilled.

YIELD: 30 SERVINGS (3/4 CUP EACH).

cauliflower

When purchasing a head of fresh cauliflower, look for a compact head with compact florets that are free from yellow or brown spots. The leaves should be crisp and green, not withered or discolored.

Microwave-baked potatoes and canned chili make my hearty dish a snap to take to the table! It's colorful, too, topped with fresh tomatoes, sour cream and shredded cheese. The no-fuss spuds are great for cookouts and picnic meals.

Laura Lunardi West
Chester, PA

chili-stuffed potatoes

PREP/TOTAL TIME: 25 MIN.

4 large baking potatoes (about 2 pounds)

1 can (15 ounces) vegetarian chili with beans

1/2 cup shredded reduced-fat Mexican cheese blend

1 cup chopped seeded fresh tomatoes

1/4 cup reduced-fat sour cream

1/4 cup minced fresh cilantro

1 Scrub and pierce the potatoes; place on a microwave-safe plate. Microwave, uncovered, on high for 12-14 minutes or until tender, turning once.

2 Meanwhile, in a small saucepan, heat chili. With a sharp knife, cut an "X" in each potato; fluff with a fork. Spoon chili over each potato; sprinkle with cheese. Top with tomatoes, sour cream and cilantro.

YIELD: 4 SERVINGS.

This hearty veggie medley has become a family staple for Thanksgiving and Christmas meals. Even though our three children are now married, when we get together for the holidays, this dish is always on the table. It's as vital to them as the turkey!

Becky Kusmaul
Ankeny, IA

vegetable stuffing bake

PREP: 20 MIN. • BAKE: 30 MIN.

1 medium onion, chopped

1 tablespoon canola oil

2 cans (10-3/4 ounces each) condensed cream of mushroom soup, undiluted

1 cup process cheese sauce

1 package (16 ounces) frozen cauliflower, thawed

1 package (16 ounces) frozen corn, thawed

1 package (16 ounces) frozen broccoli florets, thawed

1 package (16 ounces) frozen brussels sprouts, thawed and halved

1 package (6 ounces) corn bread stuffing mix, divided

1 In a large skillet, saute onion in oil until tender. Stir in the soup and cheese sauce until blended; heat through. In a large bowl, combine the vegetables and 1 cup stuffing mix. Add soup mixture and mix well.

2 Transfer to two greased shallow 2-qt. baking dishes. Sprinkle with remaining stuffing mix. Bake, uncovered, at 350° for 30-35 minutes or until vegetables are tender and edges are bubbly.

YIELD: 2 CASSEROLES (6-8 SERVINGS EACH).

colby hash browns

PREP: 10 MIN. • BAKE: 40 MIN.

1 cup milk

1/2 cup beef broth

2 tablespoons butter, melted, divided

1 teaspoon salt

1/4 teaspoon pepper

Dash garlic powder

1 package (30 ounces) frozen shredded hash brown potatoes

2 cups (8 ounces) shredded Colby cheese

1 In a large bowl, combine the milk, broth, 1 tablespoon butter, salt, pepper and garlic powder. Stir in hash browns. Heat remaining butter in a large nonstick skillet. Add hash brown mixture. Cook and stir over medium heat until potatoes are heated through. Stir in cheese.

2 Transfer to a greased shallow 2-qt. baking dish. Bake, uncovered, at 350° for 40-45 minutes or until potatoes are tender.

YIELD: 6 SERVINGS.

about cheese

Select sharp cheddar when using packaged shredded cheese for recipes that you'd like to have a bolder flavor. If you are buying bulk cheese, 4 ounces equals 1 cup shredded.

A variety of dried fruits and slivered almonds gives new life to a boxed stuffing mix in this flavorful recipe.

Taryn Kuebelbeck
Plymouth, MN

dried fruit stuffing

PREP/TOTAL TIME: 20 MIN.

1 package (6 ounces) stuffing mix
1/2 cup dried cranberries
1/2 cup chopped pitted dried plums
1/2 cup chopped dried apricots
1/3 cup slivered almonds, toasted

1 Prepare the stuffing mix according to package directions, adding the dried fruits when adding the contents of stuffing mix. Just before serving, stir in the almonds.

YIELD: 4 CUPS.

spinach supreme

PREP: 10 MIN. • BAKE: 25 MIN.

This is the best spinach recipe I've ever tasted! It's cheesy and delicious. I use the leftovers, if there are any, to make small appetizer turnovers using phyllo dough. I'm often asked for the sensational yet easy recipe.

Cyndi Gavin • Blackfoot, ID

2 packages (10 ounces each) frozen chopped spinach, thawed and squeezed dry
2 cups (8 ounces) shredded Monterey Jack cheese
1 can (10-3/4 ounces) condensed cream of potato soup, undiluted
1 cup (8 ounces) sour cream
1/2 cup grated Parmesan cheese

1 In a large bowl, combine all of the ingredients. Transfer to a greased 11-in. x 7-in. baking dish. Bake, uncovered, at 325° for 25-30 minutes or until edges are lightly browned and bubbly.

YIELD: 4-6 SERVINGS.

italian broccoli cheese bake

PREP: 25 MIN. • BAKE: 25 MIN.

1-1/2 pounds fresh broccoli spears, cut into
    1/4-inch slices

1/4 teaspoon salt

2 cups (16 ounces) 1% small-curd cottage cheese

2 egg whites

1/4 cup grated Parmesan cheese

3 tablespoons all-purpose flour

1/2 teaspoon Italian seasoning

3/4 cup meatless spaghetti sauce

1 cup (4 ounces) shredded part-skim
    mozzarella cheese

1 In a large saucepan, bring 1 in. of water, broccoli
and salt to a boil. Reduce heat; cover and simmer
for 5-8 minutes or until crisp-tender. Drain and
pat dry.

2 In a blender, combine the cottage cheese,
egg whites, Parmesan cheese, flour and Italian
seasoning; cover and process until blended.

3 Place half of the broccoli in an 11-in. x 7-in. baking
dish coated with cooking spray; top with half
of the cottage cheese mixture. Repeat layers.
Spoon spaghetti sauce over the top; sprinkle with
mozzarella cheese.

4 Bake, uncovered, at 375° for 25-30 minutes or until
bubbly. Let stand for 5 minutes before serving.

YIELD: 4 SERVINGS.

blue cheese mashed potatoes

PREP/TOTAL TIME: 10 MIN.

1 package (24 ounces) refrigerated mashed potatoes

1/3 cup crumbled blue cheese

1 Heat potatoes according to package directions; stir in blue cheese. Serve immediately.

YIELD: 5 SERVINGS.

Add your favorite cheese to homemade or prepared mashed potatoes. Prepared mashed potatoes can be found in the refrigerated meat section of your local grocery store.

Taste of Home Test Kitchen

crouton-topped broccoli

PREP/TOTAL TIME: 10 MIN.

We love this dish—even my children are crazy for it! It goes great with any meat and can easily be doubled.

Kathy Fry • Brockville, ON

1 package (16 ounces) frozen chopped broccoli

2 tablespoons water

1 can (10-3/4 ounces) condensed cream of mushroom soup, undiluted

1/2 cup shredded Swiss cheese

1/2 cup shredded cheddar cheese

1/4 cup milk

1-1/2 cups cheese and garlic croutons

1 Place broccoli and water in a microwave-safe 2-qt. dish. Cover and microwave on high for 6-8 minutes or until tender; drain.

2 Stir in the soup, cheeses and milk. Cover and microwave for 2 minutes or until cheeses are melted. Sprinkle with croutons.

YIELD: 5 SERVINGS.

super sides

Add variety to any side dish that calls for green beans, snow peas or broccoli by substituting asparagus. Be sure to adjust the cooking time accordingly.

sauerkraut mashed potatoes

PREP/TOTAL TIME: 20 MIN.

2-2/3 cups water

2/3 cup milk

1/4 cup butter, cubed

1 teaspoon salt

2-2/3 cups mashed potato flakes

1/3 cup chopped onion

1/2 cup sauerkraut, rinsed and well drained

4 bacon strips, cooked and crumbled

1 In a large saucepan, combine the water, milk, butter and salt; bring to a boil. Stir in the potato flakes. Remove from the heat and cover. Let stand for about 5 minutes.

2 Meanwhile, in a small skillet coated with cooking spray, cook onion over medium heat until tender. Stir sauerkraut into potatoes; sprinkle with onion and bacon.

YIELD: 5 SERVINGS.

Here's a classic Swiss mountain dish called Rosti. The big potato pancake is cut into wedges and usually served with bratwurst, but I have also prepared this cheese potato dish as a meatless main course. We love the nutty flavor that the Gruyere cheese provides.

Sue Jurack
Mequon, WI

swiss potato pancake

PREP/TOTAL TIME: 15 MIN.

2 tablespoons butter, divided

2 tablespoons canola oil, divided

1 package (30 ounces) frozen shredded hash brown potatoes, thawed

1 teaspoon salt, divided

1/4 teaspoon pepper, divided

1-1/2 cups (6 ounces) shredded Gruyere or Swiss cheese

Minced fresh parsley

1 In a large nonstick skillet, melt 1 tablespoon butter with 1 tablespoon oil over medium-high heat. Spread half of the potatoes in an even layer in skillet. Season with 1/2 teaspoon salt and 1/8 teaspoon pepper. Sprinkle with cheese, then top with remaining potatoes. Season with remaining salt and pepper. Press mixture gently into skillet. Cook for about 7 minutes or until bottom is browned.

2 Remove from the heat. Loosen pancake from sides of skillet. Invert pancake onto a plate. Return skillet to heat and heat remaining butter and oil. Slide potato pancake brown side up into skillet. Cook about 7 minutes longer or until bottom is browned and cheese is melted. Slide onto a plate. Sprinkle with parsley and cut into wedges.

YIELD: 6 SERVINGS.

TEST KITCHEN TIP: A nonstick skillet is a must so the pancake comes out easily.

I came up with this recipe when I tried recreating a pasta salad I had at a wedding rehearsal. It's easy to make, and I'm always asked to bring it to potlucks and parties.

Danielle Weets
Grandview, WA

pesto tortellini salad

PREP/TOTAL TIME: 20 MIN.

1 package (19 ounces) frozen cheese tortellini
3/4 cup shredded Parmesan cheese
1 can (2-1/4 ounces) sliced ripe olives, drained
5 bacon strips, cooked and crumbled
1/4 cup prepared pesto

1 Cook tortellini according to package directions; drain and rinse in cold water. Place in a small bowl. Add remaining ingredients; toss to coat.

YIELD: 5 SERVINGS.

broccoli roll-ups

PREP/TOTAL TIME: 20 MIN.

You'll need just three ingredients to make this recipe. Broccoli spears and American cheese are wrapped in convenient crescent roll dough to create the savory baked bites.

Taste of Home Test Kitchen

1 tube (4 ounces) refrigerated crescent rolls
1 slice process American cheese, quartered
4 frozen broccoli spears, thawed and patted dry

1 Separate crescent dough into four triangles. Place a piece of cheese and a broccoli spear along the wide edge of each triangle; roll up dough.

2 Place roll-ups point side down on an ungreased baking sheet. Bake at 375° for 12-15 minutes or until golden brown.

YIELD: 4 SERVINGS.

I'm always trying to get fruit onto our menus. I stirred some into plain rice pilaf one night, and it was a hit!

Lucille Gendron
Pelham, NH

fruited rice pilaf

PREP/TOTAL TIME: 15 MIN.

1 package (6 ounces) rice pilaf
2 tablespoons butter, softened
1/2 cup pineapple chunks
1/2 cup raisins
1/4 cup prepared Italian salad dressing
Toasted coconut, optional

1 Cook rice pilaf according to package directions. Stir in the butter until melted. Add the pineapple, raisins and salad dressing. Top with toasted coconut if desired.

YIELD: 4 SERVINGS.

Fresh-baked bread is easier than you think with these streamlined recipes. Fill your home with the aroma of muffins, biscuits, sweet rolls and more!

bountiful breads

This tender bread is delicious alone and even better spread with cream cheese or butter. It tastes like you spent a lot of time fussing, but it's made with convenient refrigerated biscuits.

Debbie Purdue
Westland, MI

cinnamon nut loaf

PREP: 20 MIN. • BAKE: 30 MIN. + COOLING

1/3 cup finely chopped pecans or walnuts

1/4 cup sugar

3 tablespoons butter, melted

2 teaspoons ground cinnamon

2 tubes (7-1/2 ounces each) refrigerated buttermilk biscuits

1/2 cup confectioners' sugar

1 tablespoon 2% milk

1 In a small bowl, combine the nuts, sugar, butter and cinnamon. Separate biscuits; flatten slightly. Place about 1/2 teaspoon of nut mixture on one side of each biscuit; fold other side over filling. Press edges with a fork to seal. Forming five rows, arrange biscuits folded side down in a greased 8-in. x 4-in. loaf pan. Spoon remaining nut mixture over top.

2 Bake at 350° for 25-30 minutes or until golden brown. Cool for 10 minutes before removing from pan to a wire rack. Meanwhile, in a small bowl, combine confectioners' sugar and milk; drizzle over warm bread. Cut into slices or pull apart.

YIELD: 8-10 SERVINGS.

This is a delicious and easy roll for a side dish or just by itself. Someone always asks for the recipe, so I bring printed copies whenever I take it to a potluck.

Isabel Mancini
Youngstown, OH

spinach spirals

PREP: 15 MIN. • BAKE: 25 MIN.

1 package (10 ounces) frozen chopped spinach, thawed and squeezed dry

1 cup (4 ounces) shredded Monterey Jack cheese

1 egg, lightly beaten

2 tablespoons dried minced onion

1 tube (13.8 ounces) refrigerated pizza crust

1 tablespoon butter, melted

2 tablespoons grated Parmesan cheese

1 In a small bowl, combine the spinach, Monterey Jack cheese, egg and onion. On a baking sheet coated with cooking spray, roll pizza dough into a 14-in. x 10-in. rectangle; seal any holes. Spread spinach mixture to within 1/2 in. of edges.

2 Roll up jelly-roll style, starting with a long side; seal ends and place seam side down. Brush with butter; sprinkle with Parmesan cheese. Bake at 400° for 25-27 minutes or until golden brown. Slice and serve warm.

YIELD: 14 SLICES.

go-go garlic bread

PREP/TOTAL TIME: 25 MIN.

1/2 cup butter, softened

1/2 cup mayonnaise

1 tablespoon grated Parmesan cheese

2 teaspoons minced garlic

1/2 teaspoon Italian seasoning

1/8 teaspoon seasoned salt

1/2 cup shredded Monterey Jack cheese

1 loaf French bread (about 20 inches), halved lengthwise

1 In a small bowl, beat butter and mayonnaise until smooth. Beat in the Parmesan cheese, garlic, Italian seasoning and seasoned salt. Stir in Monterey Jack cheese. Spread over cut sides of bread.

2 Place on an ungreased baking sheet. Bake at 350° for 10-15 minutes or until cheese is melted. Slice and serve warm.

YIELD: 12 SERVINGS.

red onion focaccia

PREP: 15 MIN. • BAKE: 30 MIN.

3 frozen bread dough rolls, thawed
1/2 teaspoon olive oil
2 red onion slices, separated into rings
1/2 teaspoon Italian seasoning
2 tablespoons shredded Parmesan cheese
1 tablespoon butter, melted
1/8 teaspoon garlic salt

1 On a lightly floured surface, knead dough together. Roll out into a 7-in. circle. Place on greased 7-1/2-in. pizza pan or baking sheet. Brush with oil. Top with onion slices. Sprinkle with Italian seasoning and Parmesan cheese.

2 Bake at 350° for 28-32 minutes or until golden brown.

3 In a small bowl, combine the butter and garlic salt; brush over warm foccacia. Cool for 10 minutes on a wire rack before cutting.

YIELD: 2 SERVINGS.

banana-toffee muffin tops

PREP/TOTAL TIME: 25 MIN.

2-1/2 cups biscuit/baking mix

1/3 cup English toffee bits or almond brickle chips

1/4 cup sugar

1 egg

1/4 cup heavy whipping cream

1/2 teaspoon vanilla extract

1 cup mashed ripe bananas (about 2 medium)

Additional sugar

1 In a large bowl, combine the biscuit mix, toffee bits and sugar.

2 In another bowl, combine the egg, cream and vanilla; stir in the bananas. Stir into the dry ingredients just until combined.

3 Drop by tablespoonfuls onto greased baking sheets. Sprinkle with additional sugar.

4 Bake at 425° for 11-13 minutes or until golden brown. Remove to wire racks. Serve warm.

YIELD: ABOUT 1-1/2 DOZEN.

spinach herb twists

PREP: 35 MIN. + RISING • BAKE: 15 MIN.

These impressive low-carb twists are a delicious way to serve spinach. My mom baked them when we were kids.

Amy Estes • Wichita, KS

5 cups packed torn fresh spinach

2 green onions, sliced

1 garlic clove, minced

5 tablespoons butter, divided

1/4 cup grated Parmesan cheese

1/2 teaspoon dried basil

1/2 teaspoon dried oregano

1 package (16 ounces) hot roll mix

1 cup warm water (120° to 130°)

1 egg

1 Place spinach in a steamer basket; place in a saucepan over 1 in. of water. Bring to a boil; cover and steam for 2-3 minutes or until limp. Drain well and set aside. In a small skillet, saute onions and garlic in 1 tablespoon butter until tender; transfer to a bowl. Stir in the Parmesan cheese, basil, oregano and spinach; set aside.

2 In a large bowl, combine the contents of the roll mix and yeast packets; beat in the warm water, egg and 2 tablespoons butter until dough pulls away from sides of bowl. Turn onto a lightly floured surface; knead until smooth and elastic, about 5 minutes. Cover and let rest for 5 minutes.

3 Divide dough in half. Roll each portion into a 12-in. x 10-in. rectangle. Melt the remaining butter; brush over dough. Spread spinach mixture over dough to within 1/4 in. of edges. Fold each rectangle in half lengthwise; pinch seams to seal. Cut each rectangle into twelve 1-in.-wide strips.

4 Twist strips and place on baking sheets coated with cooking spray. Cover and let rise in a warm place until doubled, about 25 minutes. Bake at 375° for 12-16 minutes or until golden brown. Serve warm. Refrigerate leftovers.

YIELD: 2 DOZEN.

These quick crescents have only four ingredients and can be whipped up in minutes. With Gouda, pecans and honey, they're super simple for a weeknight meal but are special enough for company, too.

Taste of Home Test Kitchen

nutty gouda rolls

PREP/TOTAL TIME: 20 MIN.

2 ounces Gouda cheese

1 tube (8 ounces) refrigerated crescent rolls

2 tablespoons finely chopped pecans

1 tablespoon honey

1 Cut cheese into eight 1/2-in.-wide strips. Separate crescent dough into eight triangles; sprinkle with pecans. Place a cheese strip on the shortest side of each triangle; roll up. Pinch ends to seal.

2 Place on an ungreased baking sheet. Bake at 375° for 10-12 minutes or until golden brown. Immediately brush with honey. Serve warm.

YIELD: 8 SERVINGS.

cinnamon almond braid

PREP: 20 MIN. • BAKE: 10 MIN. + COOLING

1 tube (8 ounces) refrigerated crescent rolls
2 tablespoons plus 1/4 cup sugar, divided
1 teaspoon ground cinnamon
1/2 cup finely chopped slivered almonds
1 tablespoon butter, melted
1/4 teaspoon almond extract
ICING:
1/2 cup confectioners' sugar
1/4 teaspoon almond extract
1-1/2 to 2 teaspoons milk
1/4 teaspoon ground cinnamon

1 Line a 15-in. x 10-in. x 1-in. baking pan with parchment paper. Unroll crescent dough into prepared pan; seal seams and perforations. Combine 2 tablespoons sugar and cinnamon; sprinkle over dough.

2 Combine the almonds, butter, extract and remaining sugar; spread lengthwise down the center of dough. On each long side, cut 1-in.-wide strips about 2-1/2 in. into center. Starting at one end, fold alternating strips at an angle across filling. Pinch ends to seal.

3 Bake at 375° for 10-15 minutes or until golden brown. Cool for 10 minutes; remove to a wire rack. For icing, in a bowl, combine the confectioners' sugar, extract and enough milk to achieve desired consistency. Drizzle over braid; sprinkle with cinnamon. Serve warm.

YIELD: 1 LOAF (10 SLICES).

This recipe makes great use of convenient frozen bread dough. The tender bread makes a pretty loaf to bring to a holiday gathering or to give as a gift.

Priscilla Gilbert
Indian Harbour
Beach, FL

fruit & nut bread

PREP: 15 MIN. + RISING • BAKE: 20 MIN. + COOLING

1 loaf (1 pound) frozen bread dough, thawed
1/3 cup chopped walnuts
1/4 cup golden raisins
1/4 cup raisins
1/4 cup dried cranberries
1/4 cup chopped dates
1 egg white
1 tablespoon honey

1 Turn bread dough onto a floured surface; roll out to 1-in. thickness. Sprinkle the walnuts, raisins, cranberries and dates over dough; fold over and knead well until the fruit and nuts are evenly mixed into dough. Shape into a round loaf and place in a greased 9-in. round baking pan.

2 Cover and let rise until doubled, about 30 minutes. Beat egg white and honey; brush over loaf. With a sharp knife, make 2 shallow crosses across top of loaf. Bake at 350° for 20-25 minutes or until golden brown. Transfer to a wire rack.

YIELD: 1 LOAF (12 WEDGES).

strawberry braid

PREP: 30 MIN. + RISING • BAKE: 25 MIN.

1 package (16 ounces) hot roll mix
1 cup strawberry jam
1/2 cup finely chopped dried apricots
1/4 cup chopped walnuts
1 tablespoon butter, melted
2 teaspoons sugar

1 Prepare roll mix according to directions. While dough is resting, combine the jam, apricots and walnuts in a small bowl. Turn dough onto a lightly floured surface; roll into a 14-in. x 9-in. rectangle. Place on a greased foil-lined baking sheet.

2 Spread filling down center third of rectangle. On each long side, cut 1-in.-wide strips about 2-1/2-in. into center. Starting at one end, fold alternating strips at an angle across filling. Pinch ends to seal. Cover and let rise until doubled, about 30 minutes.

3 Brush braid with butter and sprinkle with sugar. Bake at 350° for 25-30 minutes or until golden brown. Cool on a wire rack.

YIELD: 10-12 SERVINGS.

parmesan walnut muffins

PREP/TOTAL TIME: 30 MIN.

3 cups biscuit/baking mix

1/4 cup plus 1 tablespoon grated Parmesan cheese, divided

3/4 teaspoon dried parsley flakes

1/2 teaspoon Italian seasoning

2 eggs

1 cup milk

2 tablespoons butter, melted, divided

2 tablespoons chopped walnuts

1 In a large bowl, combine the biscuit mix, 1/4 cup Parmesan cheese, parsley and Italian seasoning. In a small bowl, whisk the eggs, milk and 1 tablespoon butter; stir into dry ingredients just until moistened.

2 Fill greased or paper-lined muffin cups three-fourths full. Pour the remaining butter over the tops; sprinkle with the walnuts and remaining Parmesan cheese.

3 Bake at 400° for 15-17 minutes or until a toothpick comes out clean. Cool for 5 minutes before removing from pan to a wire rack. Serve warm.

YIELD: 1 DOZEN.

These savory biscuits couldn't be simpler to make! With from-scratch flavor and a golden cheese topping, they're sure to be a hit.

Lynn Tice • Osage City, KS

caramel rolls

PREP: 15 MIN. • BAKE: 25 MIN.

Watch eyes light up at the breakfast table when you present a fresh-baked batch of my ooey-gooey treats. They're easy to fix and irresistible served warm from the oven.

Dawn Fagerstrom • Warren, MN

3 packages (7-1/2 ounces each) refrigerated buttermilk biscuits
1/2 cup sugar
1/2 teaspoon ground cinnamon
TOPPING:
1/2 cup butter, cubed
1/2 cup sugar
1/2 cup packed brown sugar
1/2 cup vanilla ice cream

1 Cut each biscuit into four pieces. Combine sugar and cinnamon. Roll each biscuit piece in cinnamon-sugar. Place in a greased 13-in. x 9-in. baking pan. In a small saucepan, combine topping ingredients; cook and stir over medium heat until the ice cream is melted and brown sugar is dissolved. Pour over the biscuits.

2 Bake at 350° for 25-30 minutes or until golden brown. Cool for 5 minutes before inverting onto a wire rack. Serve immediately.

YIELD: 12 SERVINGS.

cheese biscuits

PREP/TOTAL TIME: 25 MIN.

1 tube (12 ounces) refrigerated buttermilk biscuits
1/4 cup prepared Italian salad dressing
1/3 cup grated Parmesan cheese
1/2 cup shredded part-skim mozzarella cheese

1 Separate biscuits; dip the top of each in salad dressing, then in Parmesan cheese. Place cheese side up on an ungreased baking sheet; sprinkle with mozzarella cheese.

2 Bake at 400° for 9-11 minutes or until golden brown. Serve warm.

YIELD: 10 BISCUITS.

brown sugar

The moisture in brown sugar tends to trap air between the crystals, so it should be firmly packed when measuring. Taste of Home recipes specify packed brown sugar in the ingredients.

cherry almond pull-apart bread

PREP: 30 MIN. + RISING • BAKE: 30 MIN.

6 tablespoons butter, melted, divided
1/2 cup sugar
3 teaspoons ground cinnamon
20 frozen bread dough dinner rolls
1/2 cup sliced almonds, toasted
1/2 cup candied cherries, halved
1/3 cup corn syrup

1 Place 3 tablespoons butter in a small bowl. In another bowl, combine the sugar and cinnamon. Dip 10 frozen dough rolls in butter, then roll in cinnamon-sugar. Place in a greased 10-in. fluted tube pan. Sprinkle with half of the almonds and cherries.

2 Repeat with remaining rolls, almonds and cherries. Combine corn syrup and remaining butter; pour over cherries. Cover and refrigerate overnight.

3 Remove rolls from the refrigerator. Cover and let rise until almost doubled, about 2 hours. Bake at 350° for 30-35 minutes or until golden brown. Immediately invert the rolls onto a serving plate. Serve warm.

YIELD: 20 SERVINGS.

whole wheat
pumpkin bread

PREP: 15 MIN. • BAKE: 70 MIN. + COOLING

- 2 cups whole wheat flour
- 1 cup sugar
- 2 packages (3 ounces each) cook-and-serve vanilla pudding mix
- 1 teaspoon baking soda
- 1 teaspoon ground cinnamon
- 1/2 teaspoon salt
- 4 eggs
- 1-1/4 cups canola oil
- 1 can (15 ounces) solid-pack pumpkin

1 In a large bowl, combine the flour, sugar, pudding mixes, baking soda, cinnamon and salt. In another bowl, combine the eggs, oil and pumpkin. Stir into dry ingredients just until moistened. Pour into two greased 8-in. x 4-in. loaf pans.

2 Bake at 325° for 70-75 minutes or until a toothpick inserted near the center comes out clean. Cool for 10 minutes before removing loaves from the pans to wire racks.

YIELD: 2 LOAVES (8 SLICES EACH).

My husband, our three girls and I all love to cook, so we're always coming up with something new to try. These yummy biscuits require just four ingredients, including leftover brats. Serve them with mustard and a big bowl of rice and beans or bean soup.

Nancy Bourget
Round Rock, TX

beer 'n' brat biscuits

PREP/TOTAL TIME: 30 MIN.

  2 fully cooked bratwurst links, casings removed
  4 cups biscuit/baking mix
  2 to 3 teaspoons caraway seeds
  1 can (12 ounces) beer or nonalcoholic beer

1 Cut bratwurst into bite-size pieces. In a large bowl, combine the biscuit mix, caraway seeds and bratwurst; stir in beer just until moistened. Fill greased muffin cups two-thirds full.

2 Bake at 400° for 18-20 minutes or until golden brown. Cool for 5 minutes before removing from pans to wire racks. Serve warm. Refrigerate leftovers.

YIELD: 16 BISCUITS.

Sweet blueberries really jazz up an ordinary box of corn muffin mix. They're perfect for on-the-go snacking or as an addition to any summer potluck.

Diane Hixon
Niceville, FL

blueberry corn muffins

PREP/TOTAL TIME: 25 MIN.

1 package (8-1/2 ounces) corn bread/muffin mix
1 tablespoon brown sugar
1 egg, beaten
1/3 cup milk
1/2 cup fresh or frozen blueberries

1 In a large bowl, combine the muffin mix and brown sugar. Combine the egg and milk; stir into dry ingredients just until moistened. Fold in blueberries.

2 Coat muffin cups with cooking spray or use paper liners. Fill half full with batter. Bake at 400° for 12-15 minutes or until a toothpick comes out clean. Cool for 5 minutes before removing from pan to a wire rack. Serve warm.

YIELD: 8 MUFFINS.

EDITOR'S NOTE: If using frozen blueberries, use without thawing to avoid discoloring the batter.

crusty cheese bread

PREP/TOTAL TIME: 15 MIN.

Your family will love the melt-in-your-mouth goodness of these yummy toasted bread slices. They round out most any meal with ease.

Tanya Brady • Montague, MI

3 tablespoons butter, softened
1/2 teaspoon garlic powder
1/8 teaspoon cayenne pepper
1/2 loaf French bread (8 ounces), halved lengthwise
3/4 to 1 cup shredded part-skim mozzarella cheese

1 In a small bowl, combine the butter, garlic powder and cayenne. Spread over the cut sides of the bread; sprinkle with cheese. Place on an ungreased baking sheet.

2 Bake at 350° for 9-11 minutes or until cheese is melted. Cut into slices.

YIELD: 4-6 SERVINGS.

chocolate-pecan sticky buns

PREP: 10 MIN. • BAKE: 25 MIN.

1 can (15 ounces) coconut-pecan frosting

1 cup pecan halves

2 tubes (12 ounces each) refrigerated buttermilk biscuits

20 milk chocolate kisses

1 Spread frosting over the bottom of a greased 9-in. square baking pan. Arrange pecans over frosting; set aside.

2 Flatten each biscuit to 1/4-in. thickness. Place a chocolate kiss on one side of each biscuit. Fold edges of dough over kiss; pinch edges to seal. Arrange biscuits, flat side down, over pecans.

3 Bake at 400° for 25-30 minutes or until golden brown. Cool on a wire rack for 5 minutes. Invert onto a serving plate; serve immediately.

YIELD: 20 SERVINGS.

no nuts

If your family loves the crunch of nuts in baked goods, but someone is allergic to them, add granola or crisp rice cereal in the same amounts as the nuts. Check the cereal packages for nut allergy alerts to be certain.

poppy seed cheese bread

PREP/TOTAL TIME: 25 MIN.

1 loaf (1 pound) unsliced Italian bread
1/2 cup butter, softened
2 tablespoons mayonnaise
1 tablespoon Dijon mustard
1 tablespoon lemon juice
1 tablespoon poppy seeds
2 teaspoons dried minced onion
1-1/4 cups shredded Swiss cheese

1 Cut bread into 1-in. slices to within 1/4 in. of bottom. In a small bowl, combine the butter, mayonnaise, mustard, lemon juice, poppy seeds and onion. Spread over each slice of bread; sprinkle cheese between the slices.

2 Place the loaf in an ungreased 15-in. x 10-in. x 1-in. baking pan. Bake at 375° for 8-10 minutes or until the cheese is melted and the bread is crisp.

YIELD: 8-10 SERVINGS.

peachy rolls

PREP: 10 MIN. • BAKE: 35 MIN. + COOLING

- 2 cups frozen unsweetened sliced peaches, thawed and chopped
- 1/2 cup packed brown sugar
- 1/2 cup orange juice
- 1 teaspoon ground cinnamon
- 1 teaspoon vanilla extract
- 2 packages (19 ounces each) freezer-to-oven cinnamon rolls

1 In a small saucepan, combine the first five ingredients. Bring to a boil; cook and stir for 2 minutes. Pour into a greased 13-in. x 9-in. baking dish; top with cinnamon rolls.

2 Bake at 350° for 35-40 minutes or until golden brown. Cool for 10 minutes before inverting onto a serving plate. Drizzle with contents of frosting packets from cinnamon rolls if desired. Serve warm.

YIELD: 1 DOZEN.

EDITOR'S NOTE: This recipe was tested with Rhodes Any Time Cinnamon Rolls, which are available in foil pans in the freezer section.

I adapted a peach sauce recipe, using it on top of frozen cinnamon rolls for a quick breakfast. Fix the rolls the night before, and you can pop them into the oven as soon as you get up.

Renae Jacobson • Elm Creek, NE

ham 'n' cheese muffins

PREP: 15 MIN. • BAKE: 15 MIN.

One of my family's favorites are these muffins. The muffins not only round out most meals, but they also make great grab-and-go snacks on busy mornings.

Joy Cochran • Roy, WA

- 1/3 cup finely chopped onion
- 1 tablespoon butter
- 2 cups (8 ounces) shredded reduced-fat cheddar cheese
- 1-1/2 cups reduced-fat biscuit/baking mix
- 1/2 cup fat-free milk
- 1 egg, beaten
- 1 cup finely chopped fully cooked ham

1 In a nonstick skillet, saute onion in butter until tender; set aside. In a bowl, combine cheese and biscuit mix. Stir in milk and egg just until moistened. Fold in ham and onion mixture.

2 Coat muffin cups with cooking spray or use paper liners; fill three-fourths full. Bake at 425° for 13-15 minutes or until a toothpick inserted near the center comes out clean. Cool for 5 minutes before removing from pan to a wire rack. Serve warm.

YIELD: 1 DOZEN.

mozzarella wedges

PREP/TOTAL TIME: 25 MIN.

    1 tube (8 ounces) refrigerated crescent rolls
    1 tablespoon butter, melted
    1/4 to 1/2 teaspoon garlic powder
    2 cups (8 ounces) shredded part-skim
      mozzarella cheese

1 Separate crescent dough into eight triangles; place on a greased 12-in. round pizza pan with points toward the center. Press dough onto the bottom and up the sides of pan; seal perforations. Brush with butter; sprinkle with garlic powder and cheese.

2 Bake at 375° for 15-17 minutes or until crust is golden brown and cheese is lightly browned. Cut into wedges.

YIELD: 8 SERVINGS.

pizza sticks

PREP/TOTAL TIME: 30 MIN.

I rely on refrigerated breadsticks and pizza topping for these late-night nibbles. This is an easy snack the whole family enjoys.

Martha Riggs • Upton, KY

    1 tube (11 ounces) refrigerated breadsticks
    1/2 cup pizza sauce
    12 slices pepperoni, chopped
    12 slices Canadian bacon, chopped
    1 cup (4 ounces) shredded Italian cheese blend
      or part-skim mozzarella cheese

1 Arrange breadsticks with long sides touching on a greased baking sheet. Top with pizza sauce, pepperoni, Canadian bacon and cheese. Bake at 375° for 18-22 minutes or until breadsticks are golden. Cut apart into sticks.

YIELD: 1 DOZEN.

For mouthwatering cheesy bread that goes great with pasta or soup, this no-fuss recipe works perfectly every single time.

Brenda Jackson
Garden City, KS

savory cheese bread

PREP/TOTAL TIME: 10 MIN.

1/4 cup butter, softened

1/4 to 1/2 teaspoon lemon-pepper seasoning

1/4 teaspoon garlic powder

1/4 teaspoon dried basil

1/4 teaspoon dried oregano

12 slices French bread (1 inch thick)

2 cups (8 ounces) shredded Italian cheese blend

1 In a small bowl, combine the butter, lemon pepper, garlic powder, basil and oregano. Spread over one side of each slice of bread.

2 Place butter side up on an ungreased baking sheet. Sprinkle with cheese. Broil 4 in. from the heat for 2-3 minutes or until cheese is melted and edges are golden brown.

YIELD: 6 SERVINGS.

Soup doesn't have to simmer all day long to taste fantastic. From chowders to chilis, choose from plenty of satisfying, easy-to-make soup recipes.

sensational soups

I came up with this comforting soup when I was crunched for time and wanted to use up leftover baked potatoes. Since then, it has become a mealtime staple. Its wonderful aroma always gets cheers from my husband when he arrives home from work.

Julie Smithouser
Colorado Springs, CO

easy baked potato soup

PREP/TOTAL TIME: 30 MIN.

3 to 4 medium baking potatoes, baked

5 bacon strips, diced

2 cans (10-3/4 ounces each) condensed cream of potato soup, undiluted

1 can (10-3/4 ounces) condensed cheddar cheese soup, undiluted

3-1/2 cups milk

2 teaspoons garlic powder

2 teaspoons Worcestershire sauce

1/2 teaspoon onion powder

1/4 teaspoon pepper

Dash Liquid Smoke, optional

1 cup (8 ounces) sour cream

Shredded cheddar cheese

1 Peel and dice the baked potatoes; set aside. In a Dutch oven or soup kettle, cook the bacon over medium heat until crisp. Using a slotted spoon, remove to paper towels. Drain, reserving 1-1/2 teaspoons drippings.

2 Add the soups, milk, garlic powder, Worcestershire sauce, onion powder, pepper, Liquid Smoke if desired and reserved potatoes to the drippings.

3 Cook, uncovered, for 10 minutes or until heated through, stirring occasionally. Stir in sour cream; cook for 1-2 minutes or until heated through (do not boil). Garnish with cheddar cheese and bacon.

YIELD: 10 SERVINGS (2-1/2 QUARTS).

speedy minestrone

PREP/TOTAL TIME: 25 MIN.

2 cans (14-1/2 ounces each) beef broth

1 package (24 ounces) frozen vegetable and pasta medley in garlic sauce

1 pound smoked sausage, cut into 1/2-inch slices

1 can (16 ounces) kidney beans, rinsed and drained

1/4 cup chopped onion

1 teaspoon dried basil

1 teaspoon dried parsley flakes

Shredded Parmesan cheese

1 In a large saucepan, combine the first seven ingredients. Bring to a boil. Reduce heat; simmer, uncovered, for 10-15 minutes or until heated through. Sprinkle with Parmesan cheese.

YIELD: 6 SERVINGS.

chicken cheese soup

PREP/TOTAL TIME: 30 MIN.

4 cups cubed cooked chicken breast

3-1/2 cups water

2 cans (10-3/4 ounces each) condensed cream of chicken soup, undiluted

1 package (16 ounces) frozen mixed vegetables, thawed

1 can (14-1/2 ounces) diced potatoes, drained

1 package (16 ounces) process cheese (Velveeta), cubed

1 In a Dutch oven, combine the first five ingredients. Bring to a boil. Reduce heat; cover and simmer for 8-10 minutes or until vegetables are tender. Stir in cheese just until melted (do not boil).

YIELD: 7 SERVINGS.

new england clam chowder

PREP/TOTAL TIME: 15 MIN.

While vacationing in the New England states, we enjoyed a delicious clam chowder. When I got home, I wanted to savor the same flavor in the least amount of time. That's how this shortcut was born.

Rosann Mcwherter • Dublin, CA

1 can (10-3/4 ounces) condensed New England clam chowder, undiluted

1-1/3 cups milk

1 can (6-1/2 ounces) chopped clams, drained

2 tablespoons sherry or chicken broth

1 tablespoon butter

Shredded cheddar cheese, optional

1 In a large saucepan, combine the first five ingredients. Bring to a boil. Reduce heat; cover and simmer for 5 minutes. Sprinkle with cheese if desired.

YIELD: 3 SERVINGS.

beef macaroni soup

PREP/TOTAL TIME: 25 MIN.

1 pound ground beef
2 cups frozen mixed vegetables
1 can (14-1/2 ounces) diced tomatoes, undrained
1 can (14-1/2 ounces) beef broth
1/4 teaspoon pepper
1/2 cup uncooked elbow macaroni

1 In a large saucepan, cook beef over medium heat until no longer pink; drain. Stir in the mixed vegetables, tomatoes, broth and pepper. Bring to a boil; add macaroni. Reduce heat; cover and simmer for 8-10 minutes or until macaroni and vegetables are tender.

YIELD: 5 SERVINGS.

soothing chicken soup

PREP/TOTAL TIME: 20 MIN.

I made a few improvements to a fast-to-fix recipe to create this comforting soup. It's easy to stir up with broth, soup mix and instant rice.

Kris Countryman • Joliet, IL

2 cups sliced celery
3 quarts chicken broth
4 cups cubed cooked chicken
1 can (10-3/4 ounces) condensed cream of mushroom soup, undiluted
1 cup uncooked instant rice
1 envelope onion soup mix
1 teaspoon poultry seasoning
1/2 teaspoon seasoned salt
1/2 teaspoon dried thyme
1/2 teaspoon pepper

1 In a Dutch oven or soup kettle, simmer celery in broth until tender. Stir in the remaining ingredients. Bring to a boil. Reduce heat; cover and simmer for 6-8 minutes or until the rice is tender.

YIELD: 16 SERVINGS (4 QUARTS).

macaroni vegetable soup

PREP/TOTAL TIME: 25 MIN.

1 package (1.4 ounces) vegetable soup mix
1 envelope (.6 ounce) cream of chicken soup mix
2 cans (5-1/2 ounces each) spicy tomato juice
4 cups water
2 cans (15 ounces each) mixed vegetables, drained
Dash crushed red pepper flakes
Dash dried minced garlic
1/2 cup uncooked elbow macaroni

1 In a Dutch oven, combine soup mixes and tomato juice. Stir in the water, mixed vegetables, pepper flakes and garlic; bring to a boil. Add macaroni. Reduce heat; cook, uncovered, for 10-15 minutes or until macaroni is tender, stirring occasionally.

YIELD: 7 SERVINGS.

cauliflower ham chowder

PREP/TOTAL TIME: 25 MIN.

Even if you aren't crazy about cauliflower, you'll like this comforting, thick and chunky soup. My two daughters always did—and my husband and I love it. I found the recipe years ago, and it's great for leftover ham.

Carla Garloff • Burney, CA

2 cups sliced fresh cauliflower

1 can (14-1/2 ounces) chicken broth

1 can (10-3/4 ounces) condensed cream of chicken soup, undiluted

1 cup half-and-half cream

1/8 teaspoon white pepper

2 tablespoons cornstarch

1/4 cup cold water

2 cups cubed fully cooked ham

Sliced green onion

1 In a large saucepan, cook cauliflower in broth for 4 minutes or until crisp-tender. Stir in the soup, cream and pepper. Combine cornstarch and water until smooth; gradually stir into cauliflower mixture. Bring to a boil; cook and stir for 2 minutes or until thickened. Reduce heat. Add ham; cook and stir for 2 minutes or until heated through. Garnish with onion.

YIELD: 6 SERVINGS.

After bringing this six-ingredient soup to a teachers' function, I had so many requests for the recipe that it was published in the school newsletter. I serve the rich soup in mugs with a Caesar salad and crusty bread.

Sarah Perkins • Southlake, TX

half-and-half

You may substitute 4-1/2 teaspoons melted butter plus enough whole milk to equal 1 cup. An equal amount of evaporated milk may also be substituted.

basil tomato soup

PREP/TOTAL TIME: 20 MIN.

2 cans (28 ounces each) crushed tomatoes

1 can (14-1/2 ounces) chicken broth

18 to 20 fresh basil leaves, minced

1 teaspoon sugar

1 cup heavy whipping cream

1/2 cup butter

1 In a large saucepan, bring the tomatoes and broth to a boil. Reduce heat; cover and simmer for 10 minutes. Add basil and sugar. Reduce heat to low; stir in cream and butter. Cook until butter is melted.

YIELD: 9 SERVINGS.

My mother passed this recipe on to me. A package of store-bought ramen noodles speeds up assembly of this colorful broth with shrimp and carrots. It's delicious and so quick to fix.

Donna Hellinger
Lorain, OH

asian shrimp soup

PREP/TOTAL TIME: 15 MIN.

3-1/2 cups water
1 package (3 ounces) Oriental ramen noodles
1 cup cooked small shrimp, peeled and deveined
1/2 cup chopped green onions
1 medium carrot, julienned
2 tablespoons soy sauce

1 In a large saucepan, bring water to a boil. Set aside seasoning packet from noodles. Add the noodles to boiling water; cook and stir for 3 minutes.

2 Add the shrimp, onions, carrot, soy sauce and contents of seasoning packet. Cook 3-4 minutes longer or until heated through.

YIELD: 4 SERVINGS.

beef onion soup

PREP/TOTAL TIME: 10 MIN.

I live alone, so I'm always looking for ways to use up leftovers like beef. This soup makes a quick lunch or dinner along with fresh veggies or a crisp green salad.

Barbara Zowada • Sheridan, WY

1 can (10-1/2 ounces) French onion soup
1 cup cubed cooked roast beef
2 slices French bread (3/4 inch thick), toasted
1/3 cup shredded Monterey Jack cheese
2 teaspoons shredded Parmesan cheese, optional

1 Prepare soup according to package directions; add beef. Ladle into two 2-cup ovenproof bowls. Top each with a French bread slice. Sprinkle with Monterey Jack cheese and Parmesan cheese if desired. Broil 4-6 in. from the heat until cheese is melted.

YIELD: 2 SERVINGS.

creamy red pepper soup

PREP: 15 MIN. • COOK: 30 MIN. + COOLING

2 large onions, chopped

4 garlic cloves, minced

1/4 cup butter, cubed

2 large potatoes, peeled and diced

2 jars (7 ounces each) roasted red peppers, drained, patted dry and chopped

5 cups chicken broth

2 cans (15 ounces each) pears in juice

1/8 teaspoon cayenne pepper

1/8 teaspoon black pepper

1 In a Dutch oven, saute onions and garlic in butter until tender. Add potatoes, red peppers and broth. Bring to a boil. Reduce heat; cover and simmer for 15-20 minutes or until vegetables are tender. Remove from the heat. Add pears; let cool.

2 In a blender, cover and puree in batches. Return to the pan. Stir in cayenne and black pepper. Cook until heated through.

YIELD: 12 SERVINGS (3 QUARTS).

Everyone loves this soup's taste, but no one guesses that pears are the secret ingredient.
Connie Summers • Augusta, MI

turkey noodle stew

PREP/TOTAL TIME: 30 MIN.

For a hearty stew that comes together in a jiffy, try this one. It's chock-full of vegetables, turkey and tender noodles. It's delicious on a chilly day.

Traci Maloney • Toms River, NJ

2 turkey breast tenderloins (about 1/2 pound each), cut into 1/4-inch slices

1 medium onion, chopped

1 tablespoon canola oil

1 can (14-1/2 ounces) reduced-sodium chicken broth

1 can (10-3/4 ounces) reduced-fat reduced-sodium condensed cream of chicken soup, undiluted

2 cups frozen mixed vegetables

1/2 to 1 teaspoon lemon-pepper seasoning

3 cups uncooked extra-wide egg noodles

1 In a large skillet, cook turkey and onion in oil for 5-6 minutes or until turkey is no longer pink; drain.

2 In a large bowl, combine the broth, soup, vegetables and lemon pepper. Add to the skillet; bring to a boil. Stir in noodles. Reduce heat; cover and simmer for 10 minutes or until noodles and vegetables are tender.

YIELD: 6 SERVINGS.

This Southwestern chili full of corn is so delicious and fuss-free, I love to share the recipe. Busy moms really appreciate its simplicity.

Marlene Olson
Hoople, ND

corny chili

PREP: 20 MIN. • COOK: 3 HOURS

1 pound ground beef

1 small onion, chopped

1 can (16 ounces) kidney beans, rinsed and drained

2 cans (14-1/2 ounces each) diced tomatoes, undrained

1 can (11 ounces) whole kernel corn, drained

3/4 cup picante sauce

1 tablespoon chili powder

1/4 to 1/2 teaspoon garlic powder

Corn chips, sour cream and shredded cheddar cheese, optional

1 In a large skillet, cook beef and onion over medium heat until meat is no longer pink; drain.

2 Transfer to a 3-qt. slow cooker. Stir in the beans, tomatoes, corn, picante sauce, chili powder and garlic powder. Cover and cook on low for 3-4 hours or until heated through. Serve with corn chips, sour cream and cheese if desired.

YIELD: 4-6 SERVINGS.

cream of spinach soup

PREP/TOTAL TIME: 15 MIN.

This rich and creamy soup tastes like it's made by a professional chef. I often use drained canned spinach in the recipe, but frozen spinach works well, too.

Patricia Bradley • Rohnert Park, CA

1 package (1.8 ounces) leek soup and dip mix

1 package (10 ounces) frozen chopped spinach, thawed and squeezed dry

1 cup (8 ounces) sour cream

1/4 teaspoon ground nutmeg

Lemon slices

1 Prepare soup mix according to package directions. Stir in spinach. Cover and simmer for 2 minutes. Remove from the heat; stir in sour cream and nutmeg. Garnish with lemon slices.

YIELD: 4 SERVINGS.

basil tortellini soup

PREP/TOTAL TIME: 20 MIN.

- 4-1/2 cups chicken broth
- 1 package (9 ounces) refrigerated cheese tortellini
- 1 can (15 ounces) white kidney or cannellini beans, rinsed and drained
- 1 cup chopped fresh tomato
- 1/3 to 1/2 cup shredded fresh basil
- 1 to 2 tablespoons balsamic vinegar
- 1/4 teaspoon salt
- 1/8 to 1/4 teaspoon pepper
- 1/3 cup shredded Parmesan cheese

1 In a large saucepan, bring broth to a boil. Add tortellini; cook for 7-9 minutes or until tender.

2 Stir in the beans, tomato and basil. Reduce heat; simmer, uncovered, for 5 minutes. Add the vinegar, salt and pepper. Top servings of soup with cheese.

YIELD: 6 SERVINGS.

This soup is delicious, colorful and quick. I keep the ingredients on hand for a fast meal with a loaf of crusty bread. It's also good warmed up the next day.
Jayne Dwyer-Reff • Fort Wayne, IN

speedy vegetable soup

PREP: 10 MIN. COOK: 25 MIN.

Here is a way to make homemade soup on those hurried, hectic days. With this simple recipe, frozen mixed vegetables simmer in a seasoned canned broth for a mere 25 minutes!

Taste of Home Test Kitchen

- 1/4 cup chopped onion
- 1/4 cup chopped celery
- 1 tablespoon butter
- 1 can (14-1/2 ounces) vegetable broth
- 1 can (14-1/2 ounces) diced tomatoes, undrained
- 2 cups frozen mixed vegetables
- 1 tablespoon sugar
- 1/4 teaspoon ground marjoram
- 1/8 teaspoon pepper
- Seasoned salad croutons

1 In a large saucepan, saute the onion and celery in butter until tender. Add the broth, tomatoes, vegetables, sugar and seasonings; bring to a boil. Reduce heat; simmer, uncovered, for 20-25 minutes or until vegetables are tender. Sprinkle with the croutons.

YIELD: 4 SERVINGS.

gumbo in a jiffy

PREP/TOTAL TIME: 20 MIN.

  3 Italian sausage links, sliced

  1 can (14-1/2 ounces) diced tomatoes with green peppers and onions, undrained

  1 can (14-1/2 ounces) chicken broth

  1/2 cup water

  1 cup uncooked instant rice

  1 can (7 ounces) whole kernel corn, drained

1 In a large saucepan, cook sausage until no longer pink; drain. Stir in the tomatoes, broth and water; bring to a boil. Stir in rice and corn; cover and remove from the heat. Let stand for 5 minutes.

YIELD: 6 SERVINGS.

cowboy chili

PREP/TOTAL TIME: 20 MIN.

Busy cooks don't have time to simmer chili for hours on the stovetop. So we developed a speedy version using store-bought barbecue pork and canned tomatoes, beans and broth. Every spoonful is hearty and chunky.

Taste of Home Test Kitchen

  1-1/2 cups refrigerated fully cooked barbecued shredded pork

  1 can (14-1/2 ounces) diced tomatoes, undrained

  1 cup canned black beans, rinsed and drained

  3/4 cup beef broth

  3/4 cup chopped green pepper

  1/2 teaspoon minced garlic

1 In a large saucepan, combine all ingredients. Bring to a boil. Reduce heat; simmer, uncovered, for 10-15 minutes or until heated through.

YIELD: 4 SERVINGS.

avocado soup

PREP: 20 MIN. • COOK: 20 MIN.

Avocados are put to good use in this rich and creamy soup. I add sour cream and bacon bits to garnish the smooth sensation.

Melanie O'Shea • Saint Francis, WI

1/2 cup chopped onion

1 tablespoon butter

2 cans (14-1/2 ounces each) chicken broth

2 medium potatoes, peeled and cubed

1/2 teaspoon salt

1/4 teaspoon pepper

2 medium ripe avocados, peeled and quartered

1/2 cup sour cream

1/4 cup real bacon bits

1 In a large saucepan, saute onion in butter until tender. Add the broth, potatoes, salt and pepper; bring to a boil. Reduce heat; cover and simmer for 15-25 minutes or until potatoes are tender. Remove from the heat; cool slightly.

2 Place avocados in a blender; add potato mixture. Cover and puree. Return to the pan; heat through. Garnish with sour cream and bacon.

YIELD: 6 SERVINGS.

I enjoyed this soup in a restaurant more than 30 years ago. It was so delicious I had to ask for the recipe. Since it is simple to prepare, I make it mainly when I'm short on time or money.

Marlene Roberts • Moore, OK

avocados

To prep an avocado, cut in half lengthwise around the seed. Twist halves apart, then slip a spoon under the seed to loosen and remove. Loosen flesh from the skin with a large spoon and scoop out the avocado half.

mock chinese soup

PREP/TOTAL TIME: 20 MIN.

2 cups water

1/2 cup canned mixed Chinese vegetables, drained

1/3 cup canned cut green beans, drained

1 teaspoon chicken bouillon granules

1 In a small saucepan, combine all ingredients. Bring to a boil. Reduce heat; simmer, uncovered, for 10-15 minutes or until heated through.

YIELD: 2 SERVINGS.

quick corn chowder

PREP/TOTAL TIME: 20 MIN.

1/4 cup chopped green pepper

2 tablespoons chopped onion

2 garlic cloves, minced

2 tablespoons butter

2 cans (10-3/4 ounces each) condensed cream of potato soup, undiluted

1 can (14-3/4 ounces) cream-style corn

2 cups milk

1 package (3 ounces) cream cheese, cubed

Pepper to taste

1 In a large saucepan, saute the green pepper, onion and garlic in butter until tender. Stir in the soup, corn, milk, cream cheese and pepper. Bring to a boil, stirring frequently. Reduce the heat and simmer, uncovered, for 5 minutes or until the cream cheese is melted.

YIELD: 4-6 SERVINGS.

When time is tight, I make this savory Italian soup that relies on items most cooks have in the kitchen, including pasta, prepared spaghetti sauce, canned and frozen vegetables and frozen meatballs. The chunky mixture only needs to simmer for minutes before it can be ladled into bowls.

Beverly Menser
Madisonville, KY

pasta meatball soup

PREP/TOTAL TIME: 25 MIN.

1 cup uncooked spiral or shell pasta

1 package (12 ounces) frozen fully cooked Italian meatballs, thawed

2 cans (14-1/2 ounces each) chicken broth

1 can (28 ounces) diced tomatoes, undrained

1-1/2 cups frozen sliced carrots, thawed

1 can (16 ounces) kidney beans, rinsed and drained

1 jar (14 ounces) meatless spaghetti sauce

1 jar (4-1/2 ounces) sliced mushrooms, drained

1 cup frozen peas

1 Cook pasta according to package directions. Meanwhile, combine the remaining ingredients in a soup kettle or Dutch oven. Bring to a boil; cover and simmer for 5 minutes. Drain the pasta. Add to the soup and heat through.

YIELD: 10 SERVINGS (3 QUARTS).

vegetable cheese soup

PREP/TOTAL TIME: 30 MIN.

2 tablespoons chopped onion
1/4 cup butter, cubed
1/4 cup all-purpose flour
3 cups milk
1-1/2 cups chicken broth
1 package (16 ounces) frozen California-blend vegetables, thawed
1-1/2 cups (6 ounces) shredded cheddar cheese
3/4 cup process cheese sauce

1 In a large saucepan, saute onion in butter until tender. Stir in the flour until blended. Gradually add milk. Bring to a boil; cook and stir for 2 minutes or until thickened.

2 Stir in the broth and vegetables. Reduce heat; cover and simmer for 15-20 minutes until the vegetables are crisp-tender. Stir in cheddar cheese and cheese sauce; cook until heated through and cheese is melted.

YIELD: 7 SERVINGS.

potato leek soup

PREP/TOTAL TIME: 30 MIN.

I always like to try new and different things, and when I added a package of leek soup mix to my potato soup, my family loved it. This tasty soup even won over my picky teenagers!

Terri Day • Rochester, WA

2 cups water
2 medium potatoes, peeled and diced
2 bacon strips, cooked and crumbled
2 cups whole milk
3/4 cup mashed potato flakes
1 package (1.8 ounces) leek soup and dip mix
Shredded cheddar cheese

1 In a large saucepan, bring the water, potatoes and bacon to a boil. Reduce heat; cover and simmer for 10-15 minutes or until potatoes are tender. Reduce heat to low. Stir in the milk, potato flakes and soup mix. Cook and stir for 5 minutes or until heated through. Sprinkle with cheese.

YIELD: 5 SERVINGS.

Chock-full of healthy ingredients, this tasty soup makes a warming lunch or dinner—and it's so quick and easy to fix!

Sharon Adams
Columbus, OH

skinny tortilla soup

PREP/TOTAL TIME: 30 MIN.

1 can (16 ounces) fat-free refried beans

1 can (15 ounces) black beans, rinsed and drained

1 can (14-1/2 ounces) reduced-sodium chicken broth

1-1/2 cups frozen corn

3/4 cup chunky salsa

3/4 cup cubed cooked chicken breast

1/2 cup water

2 cups (8 ounces) shredded reduced-fat cheddar cheese, divided

28 tortilla chips, divided

1 In a large saucepan, combine the first seven ingredients. Bring to a boil. Reduce heat; cover and simmer for 10 minutes. Add 1 cup cheese; cook and stir over low heat until melted. Crumble half of the tortilla chips into soup bowls. Ladle soup over chips. Top each serving with two crumbled chips; sprinkle with remaining cheese.

YIELD: 7 SERVINGS.

From classic pasta dishes to robust casseroles, the delicious dinners in this chapter are hearty, easy to prepare and family–friendly.

memorable
main courses

Here's a tasty and elegant twist on ordinary pasta. The delicious topping of sea scallops can range from 1/2 to 1 inch thick. To cook thicker scallops more quickly, cut them in half horizontally.

Taste of Home
Test Kitchen

scallop pesto pasta

PREP/TOTAL TIME: 25 MIN.

8 ounces uncooked angel hair pasta
1/2 cup all-purpose flour
1/2 teaspoon salt
1/4 teaspoon pepper
1 pound sea scallops
3 tablespoons butter
1/2 cup prepared pesto

1 Cook pasta according to package directions. Meanwhile, in a large resealable plastic bag, combine the flour, salt and pepper; add scallops and shake to coat.

2 In a large skillet, cook scallops in butter for 2-1/2 to 3 minutes on each side or until opaque. Drain pasta; toss with pesto. Serve with scallops.

YIELD: 4 SERVINGS.

sausage & spinach calzones

PREP/TOTAL TIME: 30 MIN.

1/2 pound bulk Italian sausage
1 tube (13.8 ounces) refrigerated pizza crust
3/4 cup shredded part-skim mozzarella cheese
2-2/3 cups fresh baby spinach
1/2 cup part-skim ricotta cheese
1/4 teaspoon salt
1/4 teaspoon pepper

1 In a large skillet, cook sausage over medium heat until no longer pink. Meanwhile, unroll pizza crust; pat into a 15-in. x 11-in. rectangle. Cut into four rectangles. Sprinkle mozzarella cheese over half of each rectangle to within 1 in. of edges.

2 Drain sausage. Add spinach; cook and stir over medium heat until spinach is wilted. Remove from the heat. Stir in the ricotta cheese, salt and pepper; spread over mozzarella cheese. Fold dough over filling; press edges with a fork to seal.

3 Transfer to a greased baking sheet. Bake at 400° for 10-15 minutes or until lightly browned.

YIELD: 4 SERVINGS.

skillet shepherd's pie

PREP/TOTAL TIME: 20 MIN.

1-1/2 pounds ground beef

1 medium onion, chopped

2 garlic cloves, minced

1/2 cup water

1 envelope taco seasoning

2 cups (8 ounces) shredded cheddar cheese, divided

3 cups leftover or refrigerated mashed potatoes, warmed

1 In a large ovenproof skillet, cook the beef, onion and garlic over medium heat until meat is no longer pink. Stir in water and taco seasoning; heat through. Stir in 1 cup cheese.

2 Combine potatoes and remaining cheese; spread over beef. Broil 4-6 in. from the heat for 5-6 minutes or until golden brown.

YIELD: 4 SERVINGS.

meaty corn bread casserole

PREP: 20 MIN. • BAKE: 15 MIN.

1/2 pound ground beef

1/2 pound bulk pork sausage

1-3/4 cups frozen corn, thawed

1 cup water

1 envelope brown gravy mix

1 package (8-1/2 ounces) corn bread/muffin mix

1 tablespoon real bacon bits

1-1/2 teaspoons pepper

1/8 teaspoon garlic powder

1 envelope country gravy mix

1 In a large skillet, cook beef and sausage over medium heat until no longer pink; drain. Stir in the corn, water and brown gravy mix. Bring to a boil; cook and stir for 1 minute or until thickened. Spoon into a greased 8-in. square baking dish.

2 Prepare corn bread batter according to package directions; stir in the bacon bits, pepper and garlic powder. Spread over meat mixture.

3 Bake, uncovered, at 400° for 15-20 minutes or until a toothpick inserted into the corn bread layer comes out clean. Meanwhile, prepare the country gravy mix according to package directions; serve with casserole.

YIELD: 6 SERVINGS.

mashed potato chicken roll-ups

PREP: 25 MIN. • BAKE: 40 MIN.

6 boneless skinless chicken breast halves (6 ounces each)

1 tub (24 ounces) refrigerated cheddar mashed potatoes, divided

1 package (10 ounces) frozen chopped spinach, thawed and squeezed dry

1 cup all-purpose flour

2 eggs

2 tablespoons water

1-1/2 cups seasoned bread crumbs

1 can (10-3/4 ounces) condensed cream of mushroom soup, undiluted

1/2 cup 2% milk

1 Flatten chicken to 1/2-in. thickness. Spread 2 tablespoons of mashed potatoes down the center of each; top with spinach. Roll up and secure with toothpicks.

2 Place flour in a shallow bowl. In another bowl, whisk eggs and water. Place bread crumbs in a third bowl. Coat chicken with flour, dip in egg mixture, then roll in crumbs.

3 Place seam side down in a greased 11-in. x 7-in. baking dish. Bake, uncovered, at 375° for 40-45 minutes or until chicken is no longer pink.

4 In a small saucepan, combine soup and milk; cook over medium-high heat for 5-7 minutes or until heated through. Heat the remaining mashed potatoes according to package directions. Discard toothpicks; serve with sauce and potatoes.

YIELD: 6 SERVINGS.

seafood alfredo baskets

PREP: 10 MIN. • BAKE: 25 MIN.

- 4 frozen puff pastry shells
- 6 cups water
- 1/2 pound bay scallops
- 1/4 pound uncooked medium shrimp, peeled and deveined
- 1 cup Alfredo sauce, warmed
- 1/2 to 1 teaspoon garlic powder

1 Bake puff pastry shells according to package directions. Meanwhile, in a large saucepan, bring water to a boil. Add scallops and shrimp. Cook, uncovered, for 2-5 minutes or until scallops are firm and opaque and shrimp turn pink; drain.

2 Combine Alfredo sauce and garlic powder; drizzle over puff pastry shells. Top with seafood.

YIELD: 2 SERVINGS.

Guests will think you slaved over this sophisticated entree. But with five convenient ingredients, it goes together in a heartbeat!
Diana Smarrito • Blackwood, NJ

autumn pork tenderloin

PREP: 5 MIN. + MARINATING • BAKE: 40 MIN.

Sized right for two, this rustic and comforting entree treats you to a combination of apples, raisins and nuts. The fruited sauce adds great flavor. I serve this often, and when I double it for company, it's often greeted with cheers.

Tiffany Anderson-Taylor • Gulfport, FL

- 1/2 teaspoon salt
- 1/4 teaspoon pepper
- 1 pork tenderloin (3/4 pound)
- 1/2 cup unsweetened apple juice
- 1 cup apple pie filling
- 1/4 cup raisins
- 1/4 cup chopped pecans
- 1/4 teaspoon ground cinnamon

1 Rub salt and pepper over pork. Place in a large resealable plastic bag; add apple juice. Seal bag and turn to coat. Refrigerate for 30 minutes.

2 Drain and discard apple juice. Place pork on a rack in a roasting pan. Combine the pie filling, raisins, pecans and cinnamon; spoon over pork.

3 Bake, uncovered, at 400° for 40-45 minutes or until a meat thermometer reads 160°. Let stand for 5 minutes before slicing.

YIELD: 2 SERVINGS.

If you haven't heard of polenta before, it's made from cornmeal and can be found either on the shelf in the Italian section of your local supermarket or in the refrigerated produce area.

Taste of Home
Test Kitchen

hominy beef polenta

PREP/TOTAL TIME: 30 MIN.

- 2 tubes (1 pound each) polenta, cut into 1/2-inch slices
- 1 pound ground beef
- 1 cup chopped sweet red pepper
- 1 jar (16 ounces) picante sauce
- 1 can (16 ounces) hot chili beans, undrained
- 1 can (15-1/2 ounces) hominy, rinsed and drained
- 1/3 cup minced fresh cilantro
- 3 teaspoons ground cumin
- 2 teaspoons chili powder
- 2 cups (8 ounces) shredded Colby-Monterey Jack cheese

1 Line a greased 13-in. x 9-in. baking dish with a single layer of polenta slices. Bake, uncovered, at 350° for 15-20 minutes or until heated through.

2 Meanwhile, in a large skillet, cook beef and red pepper over medium heat until meat is no longer pink; drain. Stir in the picante sauce, beans, hominy, cilantro, cumin and chili powder; heat through.

3 Sprinkle half of the cheese over polenta. Top with meat sauce and remaining cheese. Bake for 8 minutes or until cheese is melted.

YIELD: 6 SERVINGS.

Our three kids just love the fun wagon wheel shapes in this quick and easy recipe. The mildly seasoned sauce is something that even the pickiest eaters enjoy. For variety, try it with Italian sausage instead of ground beef.

Janine Freeman
Blaine, WA

wagon train pasta

PREP/TOTAL TIME: 20 MIN.

3 cups uncooked wagon wheel pasta

1 egg

1/2 teaspoon salt

1/8 teaspoon minced garlic

1/8 teaspoon coarsely ground pepper

1/2 pound ground beef

2 tablespoons grated Parmesan cheese

2 tablespoons seasoned bread crumbs

1-1/2 cups meatless spaghetti sauce

1 cup (4 ounces) shredded part-skim mozzarella
  cheese, divided

1 Cook pasta according to package directions. Meanwhile, in a large bowl, beat the egg, salt, garlic and pepper. Add beef and mix well. Sprinkle with Parmesan cheese and bread crumbs; mix gently.

2 Crumble beef mixture into a large skillet. Cook over medium-high heat until meat is no longer pink; drain. Stir in the spaghetti sauce. Reduce heat; cover and simmer for 2-4 minutes or until heated through.

3 Drain pasta; place in a serving bowl. Add beef mixture; sprinkle with 1/2 cup mozzarella cheese. Toss until pasta is well coated and cheese is melted. Sprinkle with remaining mozzarella.

YIELD: 5 SERVINGS.

stuffing-coated chicken

PREP: 10 MIN. • BAKE: 25 MIN.

1 envelope cream of chicken soup mix

1/3 cup hot water

3/4 cup stuffing mix

2 boneless skinless chicken breast halves
   (4 ounces each)

1 tablespoon butter, melted

1 In a shallow bowl, combine soup mix and water. Place stuffing mix in another shallow bowl. Dip chicken in soup mixture, then coat with stuffing.

2 Place in an 8-in. square baking dish coated with cooking spray. Drizzle with butter. Bake, uncovered, at 375° for 25-30 minutes or until juices run clear.

YIELD: 2 SERVINGS.

tuna-stuffed portobellos

PREP/TOTAL TIME: 15 MIN.

Deli tuna salad makes these stuffed mushrooms a cinch to put together. Featuring large portobello mushrooms, it's a satisfying lunch or light supper.

Barbara Wassler • Williamsport, PA

8 large portobello mushrooms (3 to 3-1/2 inches)

1 pound prepared tuna salad

8 slices Swiss cheese

1 Remove and discard stems from mushrooms. Place caps on a greased baking sheet. Broil 4-6 in. from the heat for 4-5 minutes or until tender. Stuff with tuna salad; top with cheese. Broil 2-3 minutes longer or until cheese is melted.

YIELD: 8 SERVINGS.

My mom used to make these pork chops when I was still living at home. They boast a delicious from-scratch flavor. The sweetness of the apple mixture makes such a nice complement to the savory stuffing and chops.

Simone Greene
Winchester, VA

smothered pork chops

PREP/TOTAL TIME: 30 MIN.

1 package (6 ounces) chicken stuffing mix
4 boneless pork loin chops (6 ounces each)
1 tablespoon butter
4 medium apples, peeled and cut into wedges
1/2 cup packed brown sugar
1/4 cup water
1/4 teaspoon salt
1/4 teaspoon ground cinnamon

1 Prepare stuffing mix according to package directions. Meanwhile, in a large skillet, cook pork chops in butter over medium heat for 2-3 minutes on each side or until lightly browned. Stir in the apples, brown sugar, water and salt. Bring to a boil. Reduce heat; cover and simmer for 8-10 minutes or until apples are tender.

2 Top with stuffing; sprinkle with cinnamon. Cook, uncovered, over medium heat for 10-12 minutes or until a meat thermometer reads 160°.

YIELD: 4 SERVINGS.

grilled salmon with cheese sauce

PREP/TOTAL TIME: 30 MIN.

2 cups cherry tomatoes

4 teaspoons Greek seasoning

4 salmon fillets (6 ounces each)

1 carton (6-1/2 ounces) garden vegetable cheese spread

2 tablespoons whole milk

1 Thread the cherry tomatoes onto metal or soaked wooden skewers; set aside. Sprinkle Greek seasoning over salmon. Using long-handled tongs, moisten a paper towel with cooking oil and lightly coat the grill rack.

2 Grill salmon, covered, over medium heat or broil 4 in. from the heat for 5 minutes. Turn and grill 7-9 minutes longer or until fish flakes easily with a fork. Meanwhile, grill the tomatoes for 5-8 minutes, turning frequently.

3 In a microwave-safe dish, combine cheese spread and milk. Cook, uncovered, on high for 1 minute; stir until blended. Serve with salmon and tomatoes.

YIELD: 4 SERVINGS.

Grilled fish is accompanied by a tasty sauce made with spreadable cheese, which comes in several flavors. You can find it in the specialty cheese section of your grocery store. The creamy sauce complements the delicate flavor of the salmon, and with only five ingredients, it's super easy.

Lee Bremson • Kansas City, MO

creamy ham macaroni

PREP/TOTAL TIME: 30 MIN.

I jazz up macaroni with ham, cheese and mushrooms to make this family-pleasing fare. Sprinkle individual servings with chopped cashews if you like.

Beulah Johnston • Fort Myers, FL

2 cups uncooked elbow macaroni

1 can (10-3/4 ounces) condensed cream of mushroom soup, undiluted

2/3 cup milk

2 cups (8 ounces) shredded cheddar cheese

2 cups cubed fully cooked ham

1 jar (4-1/2 ounces) sliced mushrooms, drained

1 jar (2 ounces) diced pimientos, drained

1 Cook the macaroni according to package directions. Meanwhile, in a large saucepan, whisk soup and milk; stir in cheese. Cook and stir over medium heat until cheese is melted. Drain macaroni; add to the pan. Stir in the ham, mushrooms and pimientos; heat through.

YIELD: 4 SERVINGS.

I use my slow cooker to prepare this tender pot roast. Convenient packages of dressing and gravy combine to create a delicious sauce.

Arlene Butler
Ogden, UT

flavorful pot roast

PREP: 10 MIN. • COOK: 7 HOURS

2 boneless beef chuck roasts (2-1/2 pounds each)
1 envelope ranch salad dressing mix
1 envelope Italian salad dressing mix
1 envelope brown gravy mix
1/2 cup water

1 Place the chuck roasts in a 5-qt. slow cooker. In a small bowl, combine the salad dressing and gravy mixes; stir in water. Pour over meat. Cover and cook on low for 7-8 hours or until tender. If desired, thicken cooking juices for gravy.

YIELD: 12-15 SERVINGS.

EDITOR'S NOTE: For a filling meal-in-one, serve pot roast over mashed potatoes.

doneness test

Pot roasts are done if you can insert the tines of a long-handled fork into the thickest part of the roast easily. If the pot roast is cooked until it falls apart, the meat is actually overcooked and will be stringy, tough and dry.

alfredo seafood fettuccine

PREP/TOTAL TIME: 20 MIN.

8 ounces uncooked fettuccine

1 envelope Alfredo sauce mix

1 package (8 ounces) imitation crabmeat

6 ounces bay scallops

6 ounces uncooked medium shrimp, peeled and deveined

1 tablespoon plus 1-1/2 teaspoons butter

1/8 to 1/4 teaspoon garlic powder

1 Cook fettuccine according to package directions. Meanwhile, prepare Alfredo sauce according to package directions.

2 In a large skillet, saute the crab, scallops and shrimp in butter for 2-3 minutes or until scallops are opaque and shrimp turn pink. Stir into Alfredo sauce. Season with garlic powder. Cook and stir for 5-6 minutes or until thickened. Drain fettuccine; top with seafood mixture.

YIELD: 4 SERVINGS.

fish sandwich loaf

PREP/TOTAL TIME: 30 MIN.

1 loaf (1 pound) Italian bread

2 packages (7.6 ounces each) frozen Cajun blackened grilled fish fillets

3 tablespoons butter, melted

1 teaspoon minced garlic

1/2 cup roasted sweet red peppers, patted dry

1 cup (4 ounces) shredded part-skim mozzarella cheese

1 Cut the top half off the loaf of bread; carefully hollow out top and bottom, leaving a 1/2-in. shell (save removed bread for another use).

2 Microwave fish fillets according to package directions. Meanwhile, combine butter and garlic; spread over cut sides of bread. In bread bottom, layer fish, red peppers and cheese. Replace bread top.

3 Wrap loaf in foil. Bake at 350° for 15-20 minutes or until cheese is melted. Slice and serve immediately.

YIELD: 6 SERVINGS.

These golden tenders are cooked in just a tiny bit of oil, so there's very little fat, and they crisp up in just about six minutes.

Angela Bottger
New Canaan, CT

corn bread chicken tenders

PREP/TOTAL TIME: 15 MIN.

1/4 cup corn bread/muffin mix
3 tablespoons prepared ranch salad dressing
6 chicken tenderloins
2 teaspoons canola oil

1 Place corn bread mix and salad dressing in separate shallow bowls. Dip chicken in dressing, then roll in corn bread mix.

2 In a large skillet, cook the chicken in oil over medium heat for 3-4 minutes on each side or until meat is no longer pink.

YIELD: 2 SERVINGS.

chicken tenders

Chicken tenderloins are located under the breast of the chicken and will be weakly attached to the underside of the breast. The tenderloins are long and slender, making them perfect for frying.

puff pastry salmon bundles

PREP: 20 MIN. • BAKE: 25 MIN.

The combination of tender salmon, fresh cucumber sauce and crisp, flaky crust makes this impressive dish perfect for special occasions. Mom likes to decorate the pastry with a star or leaf design for holidays.

Kimberly Laabs • Hartford, WI

- 2 packages (17.3 ounces each) frozen puff pastry, thawed
- 8 salmon fillets (6 ounces each), skin removed
- 1 egg
- 1 tablespoon water
- 2 cups shredded cucumber
- 1 cup (8 ounces) sour cream
- 1 cup mayonnaise
- 1 teaspoon dill weed
- 1/2 teaspoon salt

1 On a lightly floured surface, roll each pastry sheet into a 12-in. x 10-in. rectangle. Cut each into two 10-in. x 6-in. rectangles. Place a salmon fillet in the center of each rectangle.

2 Beat egg and water; lightly brush over pastry edges. Bring opposite corners of pastry over each fillet; pinch seams to seal tightly. Place seam side down in a greased 15-in. x 10-in. x 1-in. baking pan; brush with remaining egg mixture.

3 Bake at 400° for 25-30 minutes or until pastry is golden brown. In a small bowl, combine the cucumber, sour cream, mayonnaise, dill and salt. Serve with bundles.

YIELD: 8 SERVINGS.

For a hot and hearty meal, try this super quick, super easy pasta dish you can fix in a flash. Serve it up with a tossed salad and bread for a fast, wholesome meal.

Taste of Home Test Kitchen

sausage 'n' black bean pasta

PREP/TOTAL TIME: 20 MIN.

- 1 package (4.4 ounces) jalapeno jack pasta mix
- 1/2 pound smoked sausage, chopped
- 1 cup canned black beans, rinsed and drained

1 Prepare the pasta mix according to package directions. Stir in the sausage and the black beans; heat through.

YIELD: 3 SERVINGS.

EDITOR'S NOTE: This recipe was tested with Lipton pasta mix.

sloppy joe calzones

PREP: 20 MIN. • BAKE: 15 MIN.

- 1 pound ground beef
- 1 cup chopped onion
- 1 cup chopped green pepper
- 1 can (15 ounces) black beans, rinsed and drained
- 1 can (6 ounces) tomato paste
- 1/2 cup water
- 1/2 cup ketchup
- 1 teaspoon dried oregano
- 1/4 teaspoon salt
- 2 tubes (8 ounces each) refrigerated crescent rolls
- 1 cup (4 ounces) shredded cheddar cheese

1 In a large skillet, cook the beef, onion and pepper over medium heat until meat is no longer pink; drain. Stir in the beans, tomato paste, water, ketchup, oregano and salt.

2 Separate crescent dough into four rectangles; seal perforations. Spoon a fourth of the meat mixture onto half of each rectangle; sprinkle with cheese. Fold dough over filling; pinch edges to seal. Cut slits in tops.

3 Place on an ungreased baking sheet. Bake at 375° for 13-15 minutes or until golden brown.

YIELD: 4 SERVINGS.

We love this south-of-the-border lasagna. The cheesy dish comes together quickly with a can of vegetarian chili. It makes a great entree served with a green salad and baked tortilla chips.

Trisha Kruse
Eagle, ID

southwest lasagna rolls

PREP: 20 MIN. • BAKE: 35 MIN.

1 can (15 ounces) vegetarian chili with beans

1 carton (15 ounces) reduced-fat ricotta cheese

1 cup (4 ounces) shredded reduced-fat Mexican cheese blend

1 can (4 ounces) chopped green chilies

1 teaspoon taco seasoning

1/4 teaspoon salt

8 lasagna noodles, cooked and drained

1 jar (16 ounces) salsa

1 In a large bowl, combine the first six ingredients. Spread about 1/2 cup on each noodle; carefully roll up. Place seam side down in a 13-in. x 9-in. baking dish coated with cooking spray.

2 Cover and bake at 350° for 25 minutes. Uncover; top with salsa. Bake 10 minutes longer or until heated through.

YIELD: 8 SERVINGS.

sausage manicotti

PREP: 15 MIN. • BAKE: 65 MIN.

1 pound bulk pork sausage
2 cups (16 ounces) 4% cottage cheese
1 package (8 ounces) manicotti shells
1 jar (26 ounces) Italian baking sauce
1 cup (4 ounces) shredded part-skim mozzarella cheese

1 In a large bowl, combine sausage and cottage cheese. Stuff into the uncooked manicotti shells. Place in a greased 13-in. x 9-in. baking dish. Top with the baking sauce.

2 Cover and bake at 350° for 55-60 minutes or until a meat thermometer inserted into the center of a shell reads 160°.

3 Uncover; sprinkle with mozzarella cheese. Bake 8-10 minutes longer or until cheese is melted. Let stand for 5 minutes before serving.

YIELD: 7 SERVINGS.

I rely on canned goods and frozen vegetables to hurry along this creamy main dish. This casserole is so popular that I always request it for my birthday dinner. Serve it with biscuits for a meal your family will love. Mine sure does!

Michelle Summers
Chattanooga, TN

veggie turkey casserole

PREP: 10 MIN. • BAKE: 30 MIN.

3 cups cubed cooked turkey

2 cups frozen mixed vegetables

2 cups frozen broccoli florets

1 can (10-3/4 ounces) condensed cream of chicken soup, undiluted

1 can (10-3/4 ounces) condensed cream of mushroom soup, undiluted

1/2 cup chopped onion

1/4 teaspoon garlic powder

1/4 teaspoon celery seed

1 In a large bowl, combine all the ingredients. Transfer to a greased 11-in. x 7-in. baking dish. Bake, uncovered, at 350° for 30-35 minutes or until heated through. Stir before serving.

YIELD: 4 SERVINGS.

hot dish tip

If you are preparing a casserole to take to a potluck or to share with a neighbor, use a fret-free disposable foil pan. That way, there's no need to worry about getting your dish back.

hot antipasto sandwiches

PREP: 15 MIN. • BAKE: 45 MIN.

2 tubes (8 ounces each) refrigerated crescent rolls

1/4 pound thinly sliced hard salami

1/4 pound thinly sliced deli ham

1/4 pound sliced pepperoni

1/4 pound sliced provolone cheese

2 eggs

Dash pepper

1 jar (7 ounces) roasted sweet red peppers, drained and patted dry

2 tablespoons grated Parmesan cheese

1 egg yolk, beaten

1 Unroll crescent roll dough into two rectangles; seal seams and perforations. Press one rectangle onto the bottom and 3/4 in. up the sides of a greased 13-in. x 9-in. baking dish. Layer with salami, ham, pepperoni and provolone.

2 Whisk eggs and pepper; pour over cheese. Top with roasted peppers and Parmesan cheese. Place remaining crescent dough rectangle over the top; pinch edges to seal. Brush with egg yolk.

3 Cover and bake at 350° for 30 minutes. Uncover; bake 15-20 minutes longer or until golden brown. Cut into eight triangles; serve warm.

YIELD: 8 SERVINGS.

Here's a rich, creamy all-in-one meal. My family just loves the easy-to-fix sauce, and it's a great way to use up leftovers from a ham dinner. For a comforting side dish, simply eliminate the ham.

Julie Jackman
Bountiful, UT

ham and swiss casserole

PREP: 15 MIN. • BAKE: 30 MIN.

- 8 ounces uncooked penne pasta
- 2 envelopes country gravy mix
- 1 package (10 ounces) frozen chopped spinach, thawed and squeezed dry
- 2 cups (8 ounces) shredded Swiss cheese
- 2 cups cubed fully cooked ham
- 4-1/2 teaspoons ground mustard

1 Cook pasta according to package directions. Meanwhile, in a large saucepan, cook gravy mix according to package directions. Stir in the spinach, cheese, ham and mustard. Drain the pasta; stir into ham mixture.

2 Transfer to a greased 13-in. x 9-in. baking dish. Cover and bake at 350° for 20 minutes. Uncover; bake 10-15 minutes longer or until heated through.

YIELD: 8 SERVINGS.

cooking pasta

To cook pasta more evenly, prevent it from sticking together and avoid boil-overs, always cook pasta in a large kettle or Dutch oven. Unless you have a very large kettle, don't cook more than 2 pounds of pasta at a time.

These recipes make supper a snap because they're all meal-in-one dishes! When time is tight, skip the pricey takeout, and turn to this chapter.

all-in-one dinners

ribbons and bows dinner

PREP/TOTAL TIME: 25 MIN.

4-1/2 cups uncooked bow tie pasta

2 pork tenderloins (3/4 pound each), cut into 2-inch strips

3 tablespoons olive oil, divided

2 cups fresh broccoli florets

2 cups fresh cauliflowerets

1 jar (15 ounces) Alfredo sauce

2-1/2 teaspoons dried basil

3/4 teaspoon garlic salt

1/4 teaspoon white pepper

1 Cook pasta according to package directions. Meanwhile, in a large skillet, cook pork in 1 tablespoon oil over medium heat until no longer pink; remove and keep warm.

2 In the same pan, saute the broccoli and cauliflower in remaining oil until crisp-tender.

3 Drain pasta; stir into the skillet. Add the Alfredo sauce, pork, basil, garlic salt and pepper. Cook and stir until heated through.

YIELD: 6 SERVINGS.

This flavorful stir-fry is easy and relatively inexpensive. It's served over ramen noodles, which is a nice change from the rice we usually have. To simplify preparation, use store-bought garlic-infused olive oil instead of minced garlic and olive oil.

Dottie Wanat
Modesto, CA

asparagus beef lo mein

PREP/TOTAL TIME: 20 MIN.

1 beef top sirloin steak (1 pound), thinly sliced

2 tablespoons olive oil

1 pound fresh asparagus, trimmed and cut into 2-1/2-inch pieces

1/4 teaspoon minced garlic

2-1/4 cups water, divided

2 packages (3 ounces each) beef ramen noodles

2/3 cup hoisin sauce

1 In a large skillet or wok, stir-fry beef in oil for 5 minutes or until meat is no longer pink. Add the asparagus and garlic; stir-fry for 2 minutes or until asparagus is crisp-tender.

2 In a small bowl, combine 1/4 cup water and 1/2 teaspoon seasoning from one ramen noodle seasoning packet; stir until dissolved. Add hoisin sauce; stir into beef mixture. Bring to a boil; cook and stir for 2 minutes or until thickened. (Discard remaining seasoning from opened packet.)

3 In a large saucepan, bring remaining water to a boil; add ramen noodles and contents of remaining seasoning packet. Cook for 3 minutes. Remove from the heat; cover and let stand until noodles are tender. Serve with beef mixture.

YIELD: 4 SERVINGS.

I was looking for a healthy alternative to beef and chicken when I found this recipe and decided to personalize it. My husband doesn't usually like fish unless it's fried, but he loves the Italian flavor in this dish. Serve it with a green salad for a great meal any time of year.

Lacey Parker
Cary, NC

tomato salmon bake

PREP/TOTAL TIME: 30 MIN.

4 salmon fillets (6 ounces each)
1 can (14-1/2 ounces) diced tomatoes, drained
1/2 cup sun-dried tomato salad dressing
2 tablespoons shredded Parmesan cheese
Hot cooked rice

1 Place salmon in a greased 13-in. x 9-in. baking dish. Combine tomatoes and salad dressing; pour over salmon. Sprinkle with cheese.

2 Bake, uncovered, at 375° for 20-25 minutes or until fish flakes easily with a fork. Serve with rice.

YIELD: 4 SERVINGS.

This must-try casserole tastes so good when it is hot and bubbly from the oven. The cheddar french-fried onions lend a cheesy, crunchy touch.

Margaret Wilson
Sun City, CA

penne and smoked sausage

PREP: 15 MIN. • BAKE: 30 MIN.

2 cups uncooked penne pasta

1 pound smoked sausage, cut into 1/4-inch slices

1-1/2 cups 2% milk

1 can (10-3/4 ounces) condensed cream of celery soup, undiluted

1-1/2 cups cheddar french-fried onions, divided

1 cup (4 ounces) shredded part-skim mozzarella cheese, divided

1 cup frozen peas

1 Cook pasta according to package directions. Meanwhile, in a large skillet, brown sausage over medium heat for 5 minutes; drain. In a large bowl, combine milk and soup. Stir in 1/2 cup onions, 1/2 cup cheese, peas and sausage. Drain pasta; stir into sausage mixture.

2 Transfer to a greased 13-in. x 9-in. baking dish. Cover and bake at 375° for 25-30 minutes or until bubbly. Sprinkle with remaining onions and cheese. Bake, uncovered, 3-5 minutes longer or until cheese is melted.

YIELD: 6 SERVINGS.

I fiddled around with this dish, trying to adjust it to my family's tastes. When my pickiest child cleaned her plate, I knew I'd found the right flavor combination.

Jennifer Trost
West Linn, OR

sausage rice casserole

PREP: 30 MIN. • BAKE: 40 MIN.

2 packages (7.2 ounces each) rice pilaf

2 pounds bulk pork sausage

6 celery ribs, chopped

4 medium carrots, sliced

1 can (10-3/4 ounces) condensed cream of chicken soup, undiluted

1 can (10-3/4 ounces) condensed cream of mushroom soup, undiluted

2 teaspoons onion powder

1/2 teaspoon garlic powder

1/4 teaspoon pepper

1 Prepare rice mixes according to package directions. Meanwhile, in a large skillet, cook the sausage, celery and carrots over medium heat until meat is no longer pink; drain.

2 In a large bowl, combine the sausage mixture, rice, soups, onion powder, garlic powder and pepper. Transfer to two greased 11-in. x 7-in. baking dishes.

3 Cover and freeze one casserole for up to 3 months. Cover and bake the remaining casserole at 350° for 40-45 minutes or until vegetables are tender.

4 **To use frozen casserole:** Thaw in the refrigerator overnight. Remove from the refrigerator 30 minutes before baking. Bake as directed.

YIELD: 2 CASSEROLES (6-8 SERVINGS EACH).

broccoli tortellini alfredo

PREP/TOTAL TIME: 20 MIN.

I indulge my weakness for fettuccine Alfredo with this trimmed-down tortellini. It has the same rich flavor without the heaviness. Nutmeg adds a lovely accent to the sauce.

Mitzi Sentiff • Annapolis, MD

1 package (9 ounces) refrigerated cheese
   tortellini

3/4 pound fresh broccoli florets

1 envelope Alfredo sauce mix

1-1/2 cups fat-free milk

2 teaspoons reduced-fat butter

1/8 teaspoon ground nutmeg

1/4 cup shredded Parmesan cheese

1/4 teaspoon pepper

1 Cook tortellini according to package directions, adding broccoli during the last few minutes. Meanwhile, in a small saucepan, whisk the sauce mix and milk. Add butter and nutmeg; bring to a boil. Reduce heat; simmer, uncovered, for 2 minutes, stirring constantly.

2 Drain the tortellini and broccoli; place in a large bowl. Stir in the Alfredo sauce, Parmesan cheese and pepper.

YIELD: 4 SERVINGS.

EDITOR'S NOTE: This recipe was tested with Land O'Lakes light stick butter.

With bacon and tomatoes, I bring the taste of a BLT to this hearty and delicious pizza. I call this "championship pizza" because it always gives our team the winning edge when it matters most.

Cindy Clement
Colorado Springs, CO

bacon-olive tomato pizza

PREP/TOTAL TIME: 30 MIN.

1 prebaked 12-inch pizza crust

1/3 cup ranch salad dressing

1 pound sliced bacon, cooked and crumbled

4 plum tomatoes, sliced

1 cup sliced fresh mushrooms

1 can (2-1/4 ounces) sliced ripe olives, drained

2 cups (8 ounces) shredded part-skim
   mozzarella cheese

1 Place crust on an ungreased 12-in. pizza pan. Top with dressing, bacon, tomatoes, mushrooms, olives and cheese.

2 Bake at 450° for 10-12 minutes or until the cheese is melted.

YIELD: 8 SLICES.

tortellini primavera

PREP/TOTAL TIME: 20 MIN.

1 package (9 ounces) refrigerated cheese tortellini
2 medium yellow summer squash, chopped
2 medium zucchini, chopped
2 teaspoons olive oil
1 pint cherry tomatoes, halved
1/2 cup chopped green onions
1/4 teaspoon pepper
1/2 cup creamy Caesar salad dressing
1/4 cup shredded Parmesan cheese
1/4 cup sliced almonds, toasted

1 Cook tortellini according to package directions. Meanwhile, in a large skillet, saute the yellow squash and zucchini in oil for 4-6 minutes or until crisp-tender.

2 Drain tortellini; place in a large bowl. Add the squash mixture, tomatoes, onions and pepper. Drizzle with salad dressing; toss to coat. Sprinkle with cheese and almonds.

YIELD: 6 SERVINGS.

au gratin ham potpie

PREP: 15 MIN. • BAKE: 40 MIN.

1 package (4.9 ounces) au gratin potatoes

1-1/2 cups boiling water

2 cups frozen peas and carrots

1-1/2 cups cubed fully cooked ham

1 can (10-3/4 ounces) condensed cream of chicken soup, undiluted

1 can (4 ounces) mushroom stems and pieces, drained

1/2 cup milk

1/2 cup sour cream

1 jar (2 ounces) diced pimientos, drained

1 sheet refrigerated pie pastry

1 In a large bowl, combine the potatoes, contents of sauce mix and water. Stir in the peas and carrots, ham, soup, mushrooms, milk, sour cream and pimientos. Transfer to an ungreased 2-qt. round baking dish.

2 Roll out pastry to fit top of dish; place over potato mixture. Flute edges; cut slits in pastry. Bake at 400° for 40-45 minutes or until golden brown. Let stand for 5 minutes before serving.

YIELD: 4-6 SERVINGS.

asian noodle toss

PREP/TOTAL TIME: 20 MIN.

8 ounces uncooked thin spaghetti
1 package (10 ounces) julienned carrots
1 package (8 ounces) sugar snap peas
2 cups cubed cooked chicken
1 can (11 ounces) mandarin oranges, undrained
1/2 cup stir-fry sauce

1 Cook spaghetti according to package directions. Stir in carrots and peas; cook 1 minute longer. Drain; place in a bowl. Add the chicken, oranges and stir-fry sauce; toss to coat.

YIELD: 5 SERVINGS.

chicken in baskets

PREP/TOTAL TIME: 25 MIN.

My family loves this quick, delicious meal. No one has to know the impressive entree starts with packaged pastry shells, canned soup and frozen chicken and vegetables.

Cheryl Miller • Robesonia, PA

1 package (10 ounces) frozen puff pastry shells
1 can (10-3/4 ounces) condensed cream of chicken soup, undiluted
1 package (9 ounces) frozen diced cooked chicken, thawed
1 cup frozen mixed vegetables, thawed
3/4 cup milk

1 Bake pastry shells according to package directions. Meanwhile, in a microwave-safe bowl, combine the soup, chicken, vegetables and milk. Cover and microwave on high for 4-5 minutes or until bubbly. Cut the top off each pastry shell; fill with chicken mixture. Replace tops.

YIELD: 3 SERVINGS.

beefy tomato rice skillet

PREP/TOTAL TIME: 25 MIN.

1 pound lean ground beef (90% lean)

1 cup chopped celery

2/3 cup chopped onion

1/2 cup chopped green pepper

1 can (11 ounces) whole kernel corn, drained

1 can (10-3/4 ounces) reduced-sodium condensed tomato soup, undiluted

1 cup water

1 teaspoon Italian seasoning

1 cup uncooked instant rice

1 In a large skillet over medium heat, cook the beef, celery, onion and pepper until meat is no longer pink and vegetables are tender; drain.

2 Add the corn, soup, water and Italian seasoning; bring to a boil. Stir in the rice; cover and remove from the heat. Let stand for 10 minutes or until rice is tender.

YIELD: 6 SERVINGS.

1 Cook spaghetti according to package directions. Meanwhile, in a large saucepan, combine the soup, water, lemon juice, basil, garlic powder, salt and pepper. Stir in the vegetables; bring to a boil. Reduce heat; cover and simmer for 3-5 minutes or until vegetables are tender.

2 Stir in chicken; heat through. Drain spaghetti; add to chicken mixture and toss to coat. Sprinkle with cheese.

YIELD: 6 SERVINGS.

corn bread hamburger pie

PREP/TOTAL TIME: 30 MIN.

This one-dish skillet supper is a big hit with children. We've added green beans and other vegetables to it, and it always turns out. To speed up prep, use store-bought chopped green pepper and onion.

Carol Ellis • Quartzsite, AZ

1 pound ground beef

1 medium onion, chopped

1 medium green pepper, chopped

1 can (10-3/4 ounces) condensed tomato soup, undiluted

1/4 cup salsa

2 tablespoons ketchup

1 tablespoon steak sauce, optional

1 package (8-1/2 ounces) corn bread/muffin mix

Minced fresh parsley, optional

1 In a 10-in. ovenproof skillet, cook the beef, onion and green pepper over medium heat until meat is no longer pink; drain. Stir in the soup, salsa, ketchup and steak sauce if desired. Meanwhile, prepare corn bread batter according to package directions; let stand for about 2 minutes.

2 Spoon over beef mixture. Bake at 400° for 15 minutes or until lightly browned. Sprinkle with parsley if desired.

YIELD: 4-6 SERVINGS.

Canned soup, frozen vegetables and other kitchen staples bring this popular family meal together in no time. Simply add a green salad and some garlic bread, and dinner is ready.

Margaret Wilson • Sun City, CA

chicken pasta primavera

PREP/TOTAL TIME: 20 MIN.

6 ounces uncooked spaghetti

1 can (10-3/4 ounces) reduced-fat reduced-sodium condensed cream of chicken soup, undiluted

3/4 cup water

1 tablespoon lemon juice

1-1/2 teaspoons dried basil

3/4 teaspoon garlic powder

1/2 teaspoon salt

1/4 teaspoon pepper

1 package (16 ounces) frozen California-blend vegetables, thawed

4 cups cubed cooked chicken breast

3 tablespoons grated Parmesan cheese

Here's a quick and simple version of the beef tips my husband loves. Even though the recipe calls for pre-made tips, the finished dish is tender and delicious. Just think— savory Stroganoff flavor with only 5 ingredients!

Pamela Shank
Parkersburg, WV

mushroom beef tips with rice

PREP/TOTAL TIME: 10 MIN.

1 cup sliced fresh mushrooms

2 tablespoons butter

1 package (17 ounces) refrigerated beef tips with gravy

1 package (8.8 ounces) ready-to-serve long grain rice

1/2 cup sour cream

1 In a large skillet, saute mushrooms in butter for 2 minutes; set aside 1/4 cup. Add beef to pan; cook for 4-6 minutes or until heated through, stirring occasionally.

2 Meanwhile, cook rice according to package directions. Remove beef mixture from the heat; stir in sour cream. Serve with rice; top with reserved mushrooms.

YIELD: 3 SERVINGS.

easy slicing

If you love fresh mushrooms but don't like to slice them, try using an egg slicer. This quick and easy method works wonders on mushrooms, making the task of slicing go much faster.

colorful chicken pasta

PREP/TOTAL TIME: 30 MIN.

1-1/2 pounds boneless skinless chicken breasts, cut into 3-inch strips

2 tablespoons olive oil

1 teaspoon lemon-pepper seasoning

1 package (16 ounces) frozen California-blend vegetables

1 can (14-1/2 ounces) diced tomatoes, undrained

1/2 cup chopped onion

1 teaspoon dried basil

1/2 teaspoon onion powder

1 package (16 ounces) angel hair pasta

Shredded Parmesan cheese, optional

1 In a large skillet, saute the chicken in oil until lightly browned; sprinkle with the lemon pepper. Add the frozen vegetables, tomatoes, onion, basil and onion powder. Bring to a boil. Reduce heat; cover and simmer for 6-8 minutes or until chicken juices run clear and vegetables are tender.

2 Meanwhile, cook pasta according to package directions; drain. Serve with chicken mixture. Serve with Parmesan cheese if desired.

YIELD: 6 SERVINGS.

scalloped potato skillet

PREP/TOTAL TIME: 30 MIN.

When we lived closer together, our family liked to get together for dinner. Every Sunday, we took turns with desserts, salads and main dishes. This is one of our favorites. Since it cooks in one pan, cleanup is a breeze.

Barbara Heile • Fortuna, CA

- 1 tablespoon butter
- 1 tablespoon brown sugar
- 1 bone-in fully cooked ham steak (1 pound)
- 3 cups refrigerated sliced potatoes
- 1 can (10-3/4 ounces) condensed cream of mushroom soup, undiluted
- 1 cup frozen sliced carrots
- 2/3 cup 2% milk
- 1/3 cup water
- 1/4 cup chopped onion
- 1/4 teaspoon coarsely ground pepper

1 In a large skillet, melt butter and brown sugar. Cut ham into four serving-size portions; discard bone. Add the ham to skillet; cook over medium-high heat for 2-3 minutes or until browned. Remove and keep warm.

2 In the same skillet, combine the potatoes, soup, carrots, milk, water, chopped onion and pepper. Cover and cook over medium heat for 10-12 minutes or until the vegetables are tender. Return the ham to the pan; cover and cook for 5 minutes or until heated through.

YIELD: 4 SERVINGS.

I first served this pasta dish with a tossed salad when friends dropped by and stayed for dinner. Since then, I've modified it to include some vegetables, so it's a complete meal by itself. My sons ask for it all the time. Frozen peas, corn, chopped broccoli and sliced zucchini can be used alone or in any combination that you like in place of the vegetable medley listed.

Amy Burns • Charleston, IL

cheese ravioli with veggies

PREP/TOTAL TIME: 30 MIN.

- 1 package (16 ounces) frozen California-blend vegetables
- 1 package (25 ounces) frozen cheese ravioli
- 1/4 cup butter, melted
- 1/4 teaspoon salt-free seasoning blend
- 1/4 cup shredded Parmesan cheese

1 Fill a Dutch oven two-thirds full with water; bring to a boil. Add the vegetables; cook for 5 minutes. Add the ravioli. Cook 5 minutes longer or until vegetables and ravioli are tender; drain.

2 Gently stir in butter. Sprinkle with seasoning blend and cheese.

YIELD: 6 SERVINGS.

shrimp 'n' veggie pizza

PREP/TOTAL TIME: 30 MIN.

1/2 cup sliced onion

1/2 cup sliced fresh mushrooms

3 asparagus spears, trimmed and cut into 1-inch pieces

1 garlic clove, minced

2 teaspoons olive oil

4 ounces uncooked medium shrimp, peeled, deveined and halved lengthwise

1 prebaked 12-inch thin pizza crust

1/2 cup pizza sauce

1 cup (4 ounces) shredded part-skim mozzarella cheese

1 In a nonstick skillet, saute onion, mushrooms, asparagus and garlic in oil until almost tender. Add shrimp; cook until shrimp turn pink. Remove from the heat.

2 Place the crust on a pizza pan or baking sheet. Spread with pizza sauce. Top with shrimp mixture. Sprinkle with cheese. Bake at 450° for 8-10 minutes or until cheese is melted.

YIELD: 6 SLICES.

This entree is a great way to showcase leftover turkey. At times, I use chicken if I have that on hand instead. Try sprinkling grated cheese over the top of each helping for extra flavor.

Peggy Key
Grant, AL

ranch turkey pasta dinner

PREP/TOTAL TIME: 20 MIN.

2-1/2 cups uncooked penne pasta
6 to 8 tablespoons butter, cubed
1 envelope ranch salad dressing mix
1 cup frozen peas and carrots, thawed
3 cups cubed cooked turkey

1 Cook pasta according to package directions. Meanwhile, in a large skillet, melt butter. Stir in salad dressing mix until smooth. Add peas and carrots; cook and stir for 2-3 minutes. Drain pasta and add to skillet. Stir in turkey; cook for 3-4 minutes or until heated through.

YIELD: 4 SERVINGS.

tasty garnishes

To spruce up any pasta dish, add a variety of toppings, such as any shredded hard Italian cheese (Parmesan, Romano and Asiago) or chopped fresh herbs (basil, chives, tarragon, oregano and/or parsley).

teriyaki salmon with sesame ginger rice

PREP/TOTAL TIME: 20 MIN.

2 cups uncooked instant rice

6 salmon fillets (4 ounces each)

1/3 cup reduced-calorie pancake syrup

1/3 cup reduced-sodium teriyaki sauce

4 green onions, thinly sliced

1 tablespoon butter

1 package (10 ounces) frozen chopped spinach, thawed and squeezed dry

1/2 cup reduced-fat sesame ginger salad dressing

1 Cook rice according to package directions. Meanwhile, place salmon fillets in a 15-in. x 10-in. x 1-in. baking pan coated with cooking spray. Combine syrup and teriyaki sauce; spoon 1/3 cup mixture over fillets.

2 Bake at 400° for 10-15 minutes or until fish flakes easily with a fork, basting frequently with remaining syrup mixture.

3 In a large skillet, saute the onions in butter until tender. Add spinach and cooked rice; saute 2 minutes longer. Stir in dressing; heat through. Serve with salmon.

YIELD: 6 SERVINGS.

broccoli tuna roll-ups

PREP: 15 MIN. • BAKE: 40 MIN.

1 can (10-3/4 ounces) reduced-fat reduced-sodium condensed cream of mushroom soup, undiluted

1 cup fat-free milk

2 cans (5 ounces each) light water-packed tuna, drained and flaked

3 cups frozen chopped broccoli, thawed and drained

2/3 cup shredded reduced-fat cheddar cheese, divided

1/3 cup sliced almonds, divided

6 flour tortillas (7 inches)

1 large tomato, seeded and chopped

1 In a small bowl, combine soup and milk; set aside. Combine the tuna, broccoli, 1/3 cup cheese and 3 tablespoons almonds. Stir in half of soup mixture.

2 Spoon filling down the center of each tortilla; roll up. Place seam side down in an 11-in. x 7-in. baking dish coated with cooking spray. Pour remaining soup mixture over top; sprinkle with tomato.

3 Cover and bake at 350° for 35 minutes. Uncover; sprinkle with remaining cheese and almonds. Bake 5 minutes longer or until cheese is melted.

YIELD: 6 SERVINGS.

Let the slow cooker do the work for you with these super convenient recipes. Most of them have a prep time of 20 minutes or less!

slow cooker cuisine

It's hard to believe something this delightful came from a slow cooker! Topped with slices of French bread and provolone cheese, individual servings are sure to be enjoyed by everyone at your dinner table.

Kris Ritter
Pittsburgh, PA

french onion soup

PREP: 15 MIN. • COOK: 8 HOURS

1 large sweet onion, thinly sliced (about 4 cups)
1/4 cup butter, cubed
2 cans (14-1/2 ounces each) beef broth
2 tablespoons sherry or additional beef broth
1/2 teaspoon pepper
4 slices French bread (1/2 inch thick), toasted
4 slices provolone cheese

1 Place onion and butter in a 1-1/2-qt. slow cooker coated with cooking spray. Cover and cook on low for 6 hours or until onion is tender. Stir in the broth, sherry and pepper. Cover and cook 2-3 hours longer or until heated through.

2 Ladle the soup into ovenproof bowls. Top each with a slice of toast and cheese. Broil 4-6 in. from the heat for 2-3 minutes or until cheese is melted. Serve immediately.

YIELD: 4 SERVINGS.

This is a very tasty and easy way to cook a turkey breast in the slow cooker. Ideal for holiday potlucks, the sweet cranberry sauce complements the meat nicely.

Marie Ramsden
Fairgrove, MI

turkey with cranberry sauce

PREP: 15 MIN. • BAKE: 4 HOURS

2 boneless skinless turkey breast halves
   (3 pounds each)
1 can (14 ounces) jellied cranberry sauce
1/2 cup plus 2 tablespoons water, divided
1 envelope onion soup mix
2 tablespoons cornstarch

1 Place each turkey breast in a 4-qt. slow cooker. In a large bowl, combine the cranberry sauce, 1/2 cup water and soup mix. Pour half over each turkey breast. Cover and cook on low for 4-6 hours or until turkey is no longer pink and meat thermometer reads 170°. Remove turkey and keep warm.

2 Transfer cooking juices to a large saucepan. Combine the cornstarch and remaining water until smooth. Bring cranberry mixture to a boil; gradually stir in cornstarch mixture until smooth. Cook and stir for 2 minutes or until thickened. Slice turkey; serve with cranberry sauce. May be frozen for up to 3 months.

YIELD: 15 SERVINGS.

chicken with mushroom gravy

PREP: 10 MIN. • COOK: 4-1/4 HOURS

4 boneless skinless chicken breast halves
  (6 ounces each)

1 can (12 ounces) mushroom gravy

1 cup 2% milk

1 can (8 ounces) mushroom stems and pieces,
  drained

1 can (4 ounces) chopped green chilies

1 envelope Italian salad dressing mix

1 package (8 ounces) cream cheese, cubed

1 In a 3-qt. slow cooker, combine the chicken, gravy, milk, mushrooms, chilies and dressing mix. Cover and cook on low for 4-5 hours or until the chicken is tender.

2 Stir in cream cheese; cover and cook 15 minutes longer or until cheese is melted.

YIELD: 4 SERVINGS.

slow-cooked taco meat loaf

PREP: 20 MIN. • COOK: 3 HOURS + STANDING

2 cups crushed tortilla chips
1 cup (4 ounces) shredded cheddar cheese
1 cup salsa
1/2 cup egg substitute
1/4 cup sliced ripe olives
1 envelope taco seasoning
2 pounds lean ground beef (90% lean)
1/2 cup ketchup
1/4 cup packed brown sugar
2 tablespoons Louisiana-style hot sauce

1 Cut four 20-in. x 3-in. strips of heavy-duty foil; crisscross so they resemble spokes of a wheel. Place strips on the bottom and up the sides of a 3-qt. slow cooker. Coat strips with cooking spray.

2 In a large bowl, combine the first six ingredients. Crumble beef over mixture and mix well. Shape into a round loaf. Place meat loaf in the center of the strips. Cover and cook on low for 3-4 hours or until no pink remains and a meat thermometer reads 160°.

3 Combine the ketchup, brown sugar and hot sauce; pour over meat loaf during the last hour of cooking. Let stand for 10 minutes. Using foil strips as handles, remove the meat loaf to a platter.

YIELD: 8 SERVINGS.

great northern bean chili

PREP: 20 MIN. • COOK: 4 HOURS

2 pounds boneless skinless chicken breasts, cut into 1-inch cubes

1 tablespoon canola oil

1 jar (48 ounces) great northern beans, rinsed and drained

1 jar (16 ounces) salsa

1 can (14-1/2 ounces) chicken broth

1 teaspoon ground cumin, optional

2 cups (8 ounces) shredded Monterey Jack cheese

1 In a large skillet, brown chicken in oil; drain. In a 4- or 5-qt. slow cooker, combine the beans, salsa, broth, cumin if desired and chicken. Cover and cook on low for 4-6 hours or until chicken is tender. Serve with cheese.

YIELD: 8 SERVINGS.

italian appetizer meatballs

PREP: 40 MIN. • COOK: 2 HOURS

Store-bought spaghetti sauce speeds up the preparation of my homemade meatball appetizers. Leftovers make terrific sub sandwiches.

Rene McCrory • Indianapolis, IN

- 2 eggs, lightly beaten
- 1/2 cup dry bread crumbs
- 1/4 cup whole milk
- 2 teaspoons grated Parmesan cheese
- 1 teaspoon salt
- 1/4 teaspoon pepper
- 1/8 teaspoon garlic powder
- 1 pound ground beef
- 1 pound bulk Italian sausage
- 2 jars (26 ounces each) spaghetti sauce

1 In a large bowl, combine the first seven ingredients. Crumble beef and sausage over mixture and mix well. Shape into 1-in. balls.

2 Place meatballs on a greased rack in a shallow baking pan. Bake, uncovered, at 400° for 15-20 minutes or until no longer pink.

3 Transfer meatballs to a 4-qt. slow cooker; add spaghetti sauce. Cover and cook on high for 2-3 hours or until heated through.

YIELD: 4 DOZEN.

> Being an at-home parent as well as helping my husband on our ranch, I'm always looking for simple meals for the slow cooker. My family really likes this hearty main dish.
>
> Colleen Faber • Buffalo, MT

meatball tip

For meatballs to cook evenly, it's important for them to be the same size. The easiest way to do this is by using a 1- or 1-1/2-inch cookie scoop. Scoop the meat mixture and level off the top. Gently roll into a ball.

soy-garlic chicken

PREP: 10 MIN. • COOK: 4 HOURS

- 6 chicken leg quarters, skin removed
- 1 can (8 ounces) tomato sauce
- 1/2 cup soy sauce
- 1/4 cup packed brown sugar
- 2 teaspoons minced garlic

1 With a sharp knife, cut the leg quarters at the joints if desired. Place in a 4-qt. slow cooker. In a small bowl, combine the tomato sauce, soy sauce, brown sugar and garlic; pour over chicken. Cover and cook on low for 4-5 hours or until a meat thermometer reads 180°.

YIELD: 6 SERVINGS.

maple baked beans

PREP: 15 MIN. • COOK: 6 HOURS

3 cans (15 ounces each) pork and beans
1/2 cup finely chopped onion
1/2 cup chopped green pepper
1/2 cup ketchup
1/2 cup maple syrup
2 tablespoons finely chopped seeded jalapeno pepper
1/2 cup crumbled cooked bacon

1 In a 3-qt. slow cooker, combine the first six ingredients. Cover and cook on low for 6-7 hours or until vegetables are tender. Just before serving, stir in bacon.

YIELD: 8 SERVINGS.

EDITOR'S NOTE: We recommend wearing disposable gloves when cutting hot peppers. Avoid touching your face.

baked bacon

Instead of frying bacon, lay strips on a jelly roll pan and bake at 350° for about 30 minutes. Prepared this way, bacon comes out crisp and flat. Plus the pan cleans easily, so there's no stovetop spattering.

My husband and I both work full time and we have three daughters, so quick meals are important. This stew consistently tastes great, making it one of our regular menu items.

Marie Shanks
Terre Haute, IN

home-style stew

PREP: 20 MIN. • COOK: 6 HOURS

2 packages (16 ounces each) frozen vegetables for stew

1-1/2 pounds beef stew meat, cut into 1-inch cubes

1 can (10-3/4 ounces) condensed cream of mushroom soup, undiluted

1 can (10-3/4 ounces) condensed tomato soup, undiluted

1 envelope reduced-sodium onion soup mix

1 Place vegetables in a 5-qt. slow cooker. In a large nonstick skillet coated with cooking spray, brown beef on all sides.

2 Transfer to slow cooker. Combine the remaining ingredients; pour over top.

3 Cover and cook on low for 6-8 hours or until beef is tender.

YIELD: 5 SERVINGS.

hash browns with ham

PREP: 15 MIN. • COOK: 3-1/4 HOURS

1 package (32 ounces) frozen cubed hash brown potatoes, thawed

1 cup cubed fully cooked ham

1 small onion, chopped

2 cups (8 ounces) shredded cheddar cheese, divided

1 can (14-3/4 ounces) condensed cream of chicken soup, undiluted

1/2 cup butter, melted

1 cup (8 ounces) sour cream

1 In a 3-qt. slow cooker, combine the potatoes, ham, onion and 1 cup cheese. Combine soup and butter; pour over potato mixture. Cover and cook on low for 3-4 hours or until potatoes are tender.

2 Stir in the sour cream. Sprinkle with remaining cheese. Cover and cook for 15 minutes or until cheese is melted.

YIELD: 8 SERVINGS.

With just 15 minutes of prep, you'll be out of the kitchen in no time. It gets even better served with sour cream and chopped cilantro. Reduced-fat ingredients don't make it any less delicious.

Brandi Castillo
Santa Maria, CA

slow-cooked southwest chicken

PREP: 15 MIN. • COOK: 6 HOURS

2 cans (15 ounces each) black beans, rinsed and drained

1 can (14-1/2 ounces) reduced-sodium chicken broth

1 can (14-1/2 ounces) diced tomatoes with mild green chilies, undrained

1/2 pound boneless skinless chicken breast

1 jar (8 ounces) chunky salsa

1 cup frozen corn

1 tablespoon dried parsley flakes

1 teaspoon ground cumin

1/4 teaspoon pepper

3 cups hot cooked rice

1 In a 2- or 3-qt. slow cooker, combine the beans, broth, tomatoes, chicken, salsa, corn and seasonings. Cover and cook on low for 6-8 hours or until a meat thermometer reads 170°.

2 Shred chicken with two forks and return to the slow cooker; heat through. Serve with rice.

YIELD: 6 SERVINGS.

Oatmeal fans will love this dish. Although the pears, blueberries and granola make a beautiful breakfast, it also makes a delicious dessert when served with vanilla ice cream.

Lisa Workman • Boones Mill, VA

pear-blueberry granola

PREP: 15 MIN. • COOK: 3 HOURS

5 medium pears, peeled and thinly sliced
2 cups fresh or frozen unsweetened blueberries
1/2 cup packed brown sugar
1/3 cup apple cider or unsweetened apple juice
1 tablespoon all-purpose flour
1 tablespoon lemon juice
2 teaspoons ground cinnamon
2 tablespoons butter
3 cups granola without raisins

1 In a 4-qt. slow cooker, combine the first seven ingredients. Dot with butter. Sprinkle granola over top. Cover and cook on low for 3-4 hours or until fruit is tender.

YIELD: 10 SERVINGS.

baby back ribs

PREP: 5 MIN. • COOK: 6-1/4 HOURS

Slow-cook the ribs during the day, and they will be ready to finish on the grill when you get home.

Taste of Home Test Kitchen

2-1/2 pounds pork baby back ribs, cut into eight pieces
5 cups water
1 medium onion, sliced
2 celery ribs, cut in half
2 teaspoons minced garlic, divided
1 teaspoon whole peppercorns
1/2 cup barbecue sauce
1/4 cup plum sauce
Dash hot pepper sauce

1 Place the ribs in a 5-qt. slow cooker. Add the water, onion, celery, 1 teaspoon garlic and peppercorns. Cover and cook on low for 6 hours or until the meat is tender.

2 In a small saucepan, combine the barbecue sauce, plum sauce, hot pepper sauce and remaining garlic. Cook and stir over medium heat for 5 minutes or until heated through. Remove ribs from slow cooker. Discard cooking juices and vegetables.

3 Using long-handled tongs, moisten a paper towel with cooking oil and lightly coat the grill rack. Brush ribs with sauce. Grill, uncovered, over medium-low heat for 8-10 minutes or until browned, turning occasionally and brushing with remaining sauce.

YIELD: 4 SERVINGS.

about pears

Purchase pears that are firm, fragrant and free of blemishes or soft spots. For fresh pear halves, a melon baller is the perfect tool for removing the core.

This comforting side dish is convenient to make in the slow cooker when your oven and stovetop are occupied with other dishes. The warm medley also can be served over sliced pound cake for dessert.

Debbie Kimbrough
Lexington, MS

hot fruit salad

PREP: 10 MIN. • COOK: 2 HOURS

- 3/4 cup sugar
- 1/2 cup butter, melted
- 1/4 teaspoon ground cinnamon
- 1/4 teaspoon ground nutmeg
- 1/8 teaspoon salt
- 2 cans (15-1/4 ounces each) sliced peaches, drained
- 2 cans (15-1/4 ounces each) sliced pears, undrained
- 1 jar (23 ounces) chunky applesauce
- 1/2 cup dried apricots, chopped
- 1/4 cup dried cranberries

1 In a 3-qt. slow cooker, combine the sugar, butter, cinnamon, nutmeg and salt. Stir in the remaining ingredients. Cover and cook on high for 2 hours or until heated through.

YIELD: 10 SERVINGS.

herbed chicken and tomatoes

PREP: 5 MIN. • COOK: 5 HOURS

I put a tangy spin on chicken by adding just a few easy ingredients. Recipes such as this are really a plus when you work a full-time job but still want to put a healthy, satisfying meal on the table.

Rebecca Popke • Largo, FL

- 1 pound boneless skinless chicken breasts, cut into 1-1/2-inch pieces
- 2 cans (14-1/2 ounces each) Italian diced tomatoes
- 1 envelope savory herb with garlic soup mix
- 1/4 teaspoon sugar
- Hot cooked pasta
- Shredded Parmesan cheese

1 In a 3-qt. slow cooker, combine the chicken, tomatoes, soup mix and sugar. Cover and cook on low for 5-6 hours or until chicken is no longer pink. Serve with pasta; sprinkle with cheese.

YIELD: 4 SERVINGS.

This is one of my all-time favorite slow cooker recipes! With 28 grams of protein per serving, it is a great way to meet your daily protein needs!

Jami Hilker
Harrison, AR

italian beef on rolls

PREP: 15 MIN. • COOK: 8 HOURS

1 beef sirloin tip roast (2 pounds)
1 can (14-1/2 ounces) diced tomatoes, undrained
1 medium green pepper, chopped
1/2 cup water
1 tablespoon sesame seeds
1-1/2 teaspoons garlic powder
1 teaspoon fennel seed, crushed
1/2 teaspoon salt
1/2 teaspoon pepper
8 hard rolls, split

1 Place the roast in a 3-qt. slow cooker. In a small bowl, combine the tomatoes, green pepper, water, sesame seeds and seasonings; pour over the roast. Cover and cook on low for 8-9 hours or until the meat is tender.

2 Remove roast; cool slightly. Skim fat from cooking juices; shred beef and return to the slow cooker. Serve on rolls.

YIELD: 8 SERVINGS.

EDITOR'S NOTE: For Stovetop Italian Beef on Rolls, place the roast in a Dutch oven. Pour tomato mixture over the top. Bring to a boil. Reduce heat; cover and simmer for 1-1/2 to 2 hours or until meat is very tender. Proceed as directed. Spicy Italian Beef: Add 1 chopped jalapeno pepper or 1/2 teaspoon crushed red pepper along with the other seasonings to the slow cooker.

A comforting casserole with mass appeal is just what you need when cooking for a crowd. For added convenience, it stays warm in a slow cooker.

Virginia Krites
Cridersville, OH

slow cooker pizza casserole

PREP: 20 MIN. • COOK: 2 HOURS

1 package (16 ounces) rigatoni or large tube pasta

1-1/2 pounds ground beef

1 small onion, chopped

4 cups (16 ounces) shredded part-skim mozzarella cheese

2 cans (15 ounces each) pizza sauce

1 can (10-3/4 ounces) condensed cream of mushroom soup, undiluted

1 package (8 ounces) sliced pepperoni

1 Cook pasta according to package directions. Meanwhile, in a skillet, cook beef and onion over medium heat until meat is no longer pink; drain.

2 Drain pasta; place in a 5-qt. slow cooker. Stir in the beef mixture, cheese, pizza sauce, soup and pepperoni. Cover and cook on low for 2-3 hours or until heated through and the cheese is melted.

YIELD: 12-14 SERVINGS.

hot caramel apples

PREP: 15 MIN. • COOK: 4 HOURS

Who ever thinks of making dessert in a slow cooker? This old-time favorite goes together quickly, and it's a treat to come home to the comforting aroma of cinnamony baked apples.

Pat Sparks • St. Charles, MO

4 large tart apples, cored

1/2 cup apple juice

1/2 cup packed brown sugar

12 red-hot candies

1/4 cup butter

8 caramels

1/4 teaspoon ground cinnamon

Whipped cream, optional

1 Peel about 3/4 in. off the top of each apple; place in a 3-qt. slow cooker. Pour juice over apples. Fill the center of each apple with 2 tablespoons of sugar, three red-hots, 1 tablespoon butter and two caramels. Sprinkle with cinnamon.

2 Cover and cook on low for 4-6 hours or until the apples are tender. Serve immediately with whipped cream if desired.

YIELD: 4 SERVINGS.

tender pork chops

PREP: 20 MIN. • COOK: 6 HOURS

1/2 cup all-purpose flour

1-1/2 teaspoons ground mustard

1 teaspoon seasoned salt

1/2 teaspoon garlic powder

6 bone-in pork loin chops (1 inch thick and 8 ounces each)

2 tablespoons canola oil

1 can (10-1/2 ounces) condensed chicken with rice soup, undiluted

1 In a large resealable plastic bag, combine the flour, mustard, seasoned salt and garlic powder. Add pork chops, one at a time, and shake to coat.

2 In a large skillet, brown chops in oil on both sides. Place in a 3-qt. slow cooker. Pour soup over pork. Cover and cook on low for 6-7 hours or until meat is tender.

YIELD: 6 SERVINGS.

slow-cooked turkey sandwiches

PREP: 15 MIN. • COOK: 3 HOURS

These sandwiches have been such a hit at office potlucks that I keep copies of the recipe in my desk to hand out.

Diane Twait Nelsen • Ringsted, IA

6 cups cubed cooked turkey

2 cups cubed process cheese (Velveeta)

1 can (10-3/4 ounces) condensed cream of chicken soup, undiluted

1 can (10-3/4 ounces) condensed cream of mushroom soup, undiluted

1/2 cup finely chopped onion

1/2 cup chopped celery

22 wheat sandwich buns, split

1 In a 3-qt. slow cooker, combine the first six ingredients. Cover and cook on low for 3-4 hours or until onion and celery are tender and cheese is melted. Stir mixture before spooning 1/2 cup onto each bun.

YIELD: 22 SERVINGS.

It's the slow cooking of this brisket that makes it so tender. It gets a wonderfully sweet-tangy flavor from chili sauce, cider vinegar and brown sugar.

Elaine Sweet
Dallas, TX

double-onion beef brisket

PREP: 25 MIN. • COOK: 6 HOURS

1 fresh beef brisket (4 pounds)
1-1/2 teaspoons kosher salt
1-1/2 teaspoons coarsely ground pepper
2 tablespoons olive oil
3 medium onions, halved and sliced
3 celery ribs, chopped
1 cup chili sauce
1/4 cup packed brown sugar
1/4 cup cider vinegar
1 envelope onion soup mix

1 Cut brisket in half; sprinkle all sides with salt and pepper. In a large skillet, brown brisket in oil; remove and set aside. In the same skillet, cook and stir onions on low heat for 8-10 minutes or until they are caramelized.

2 Place half of the onions in a 5-qt. slow cooker; top with celery and brisket. Combine the chili sauce, brown sugar, vinegar and soup mix. Pour over brisket; top with remaining onions.

3 Cover and cook on low for 6-7 hours or until meat is tender. Let stand for 5 minutes before slicing. Skim fat from cooking juices and serve with meat.

YIELD: 10 SERVINGS.

EDITOR'S NOTE: This is a fresh beef brisket, not corned beef.

These dazzling sweets are quick and easy to make!

delectable desserts

gooey chocolate cookies

PREP: 15 MIN. + CHILLING • BAKE: 10 MIN./BATCH

1 package (8 ounces) cream cheese, softened
1/2 cup butter, softened
1 egg
1 teaspoon vanilla extract
1 package (18-1/4 ounces) chocolate cake mix

1 In a large bowl, beat cream cheese and butter until light and fluffy. Beat in egg and vanilla. Add cake mix and mix well (dough will be sticky). Cover and refrigerate for 2 hours.

2 Roll rounded tablespoonfuls of dough into balls. Place 2 in. apart on ungreased baking sheets. Bake at 350° for 9-11 minutes or until tops are cracked. Cool for 2 minutes before removing from pans to wire racks.

YIELD: 4-1/2 DOZEN.

With chocolate sauce designs piped on top, these sensational squares promise to garner a lot of attention! Best of all, you'll be amazed at how easy these rich desserts are to assemble.

Laurene Hunsicker
Canton, PA

patterned cheesecake squares

PREP: 15 MIN. • BAKE: 45 MIN. + COOLING

1 tube (16-1/2 ounces) refrigerated peanut butter cookie dough
1 package (8 ounces) cream cheese, softened
1/4 cup sugar
1 cup (8 ounces) sour cream
1 egg
1/2 teaspoon vanilla extract
1-1/4 cups chocolate ice cream topping, divided

1 Cut cookie dough into 24 slices. Arrange side by side in an ungreased 13-in. x 9-in. baking pan; press together to close gaps. Bake at 350° for 12-14 minutes or until lightly browned.

2 Meanwhile, in a large bowl, beat cream cheese and sugar until smooth. Beat in the sour cream, egg and vanilla and mix well. Spread 3/4 cup chocolate topping over warm crust. Carefully spread cream cheese mixture evenly over topping.

3 Bake for 30-35 minutes or until a toothpick inserted near the center comes out clean. Cool on a wire rack. Cut into bars.

4 Place remaining chocolate topping in a heavy-duty resealable plastic bag and cut a small hole in the corner of bag. Pipe patterns on bars. Refrigerate until serving.

YIELD: 2 DOZEN.

peanut butter chocolate cake

PREP: 35 MIN. • BAKE: 35 MIN. + COOLING

1 package (18-1/4 ounces) chocolate cake mix
1-1/4 cups water
1/2 cup reduced-fat sour cream
2 egg whites
1 package (8 ounces) reduced-fat cream cheese
1 egg, lightly beaten
1/2 cup sugar
1/2 cup reduced-fat creamy peanut butter
1/4 cup fat-free milk

1 In a large bowl, beat the cake mix, water, sour cream and egg whites on medium speed for 2 minutes. Coat a 13-in. x 9-in. baking pan with cooking spray and dust with flour. Pour the batter into the pan.

2 In a small bowl, beat the cream cheese, egg, sugar, peanut butter and milk until smooth. Drop by tablespoonfuls over batter and swirl with a knife. Bake at 350° for 35-40 minutes or until a toothpick inserted near the center comes out clean. Cool on a wire rack. Refrigerate leftovers.

YIELD: 18 SERVINGS.

brickle cookies

PREP/TOTAL TIME: 25 MIN.

The only problem with these cookies? Once you eat one, you want more!

Robert Moon • Tampa, FL

1 package (9 ounces) yellow cake mix
1/4 cup vegetable oil
1 egg, lightly beaten
1/2 teaspoon vanilla extract
1/2 cup chopped pecans
1/2 cup almond brickle chips or English toffee bits

1 In a bowl, combine the dry cake mix, vegetable oil, egg and vanilla; mix well. Stir in pecans. Refrigerate for 1 hour or until firm enough to handle.

2 Roll into 1-in. balls; dip top of each ball into toffee bits and set 2 in. apart on greased baking sheets. Bake at 350° for 10-12 minutes or until golden brown. Cool for 3 minutes before removing to wire racks.

YIELD: ABOUT 1-1/2 DOZEN.

fluffy chocolate pie

PREP: 15 MIN. + CHILLING

2-1/2 cups miniature milk chocolate kisses
1 carton (12 ounces) frozen whipped topping, thawed, divided
1 graham cracker crust (9 inches)
20 miniature peanut butter cups, chopped

1 In a large microwave-safe bowl, melt chocolate kisses; stir until smooth. Cool slightly. Fold in 3-1/2 cups whipped topping until blended.

2 Spread half of the chocolate mixture into crust; sprinkle with peanut butter cups. Top with remaining chocolate mixture. Chill for at least 30 minutes. Top with remaining whipped topping.

YIELD: 8 SERVINGS.

boston cream angel cake

PREP: 10 MIN. + CHILLING

2 cups plus 1 tablespoon cold milk, divided

1 package (3.4 ounces) instant French vanilla pudding mix

1 prepared angel food cake (8 to 10 ounces)

1 cup hot fudge ice cream topping

1 In a large bowl, whisk 2 cups milk and pudding mix for 2 minutes. Let stand for 2 minutes or until soft-set. Split cake into three horizontal layers; place bottom layer on a serving plate. Spread with half of the pudding. Repeat layers. Replace cake top. Cover and refrigerate until serving.

2 In a small microwave-safe bowl, heat hot fudge topping; stir in remaining milk. Drizzle over cake, allowing it to drip down the sides. Refrigerate leftovers.

YIELD: 8 SERVINGS.

devil's food caramel torte

PREP: 40 MIN. • BAKE: 25 MIN. + COOLING

My family calls this festive dessert "turtle cake" because of the delectable candy bits in the moist cake layers and the gooey-good filling. It is an impressive-looking cake but quite easy to make, as you'll see from the recipe.

Dianne Bettin • Truman, MN

- 1 package (18-1/4 ounces) devil's food cake mix
- 1 cup buttermilk
- 1/2 cup canola oil
- 3 eggs
- 1 package (7 ounces) milk chocolate turtle candies, chopped, divided
- 1 tablespoon baking cocoa
- 1-1/2 cups heavy whipping cream
- 1/3 cup caramel ice cream topping
- 1 can (16 ounces) chocolate frosting
- Additional milk chocolate turtle candies, broken, optional

1 Line two 9-in. round baking pans with waxed paper; grease the paper and set aside. In a large bowl, combine the cake mix, buttermilk, oil and eggs. Beat on low speed for 30 seconds. Beat on medium for 2 minutes. Combine 1 cup candies and cocoa; fold into batter.

2 Pour into prepared pans. Bake at 350° for 25-30 minutes or until a toothpick inserted near the center comes out clean. Cool for 10 minutes before removing from pans to wire racks to cool completely. Remove waxed paper.

3 In a small bowl, beat cream until it begins to thicken. Add caramel topping; beat until stiff peaks form. Fold in remaining candies.

4 Place one cake layer on a serving plate; spread with chocolate frosting. Top with remaining cake layer; frost top and sides of torte with cream mixture. Garnish with additional candies if desired. Refrigerate until serving.

YIELD: 12 SERVINGS.

This is so quick, you'll have it ready in less than 10 minutes. And it is so good!
Cathy Shortall • Easton, MD

easy cheesecake pie

PREP/TOTAL TIME: 5 MIN. + CHILLING

- 1 carton (24.3 ounces) ready-to-serve cheesecake filling
- 1-1/2 cups coarsely crushed cream-filled chocolate sandwich cookies (about 12 cookies), divided
- 1 chocolate crumb crust (9 inches)

1 In a large bowl, combine cheesecake filling and 1-1/4 cups cookie crumbs. Spoon into crust; sprinkle with remaining crumbs. Chill until serving.

YIELD: 8 SERVINGS.

mint dip with brownies

PREP: 15 MIN. • BAKE: 30 MIN. + COOLING

- 1 package fudge brownie mix (8-inch square pan size)
- 3/4 cup sour cream
- 2 tablespoons brown sugar
- 2 tablespoons green creme de menthe

1 Prepare and bake the brownies according to package directions. Cool on a wire rack. Meanwhile, in a small bowl, combine the sour cream, brown sugar and creme de menthe; cover and refrigerate until serving.

2 Cut the brownies into 1-in. diamonds. Serve with the mint dip.

YIELD: 1 DOZEN (3/4 CUP DIP).

My sister shared this simple recipe with me many years ago. The cool, refreshing dip also tastes terrific with fresh strawberries.
Carol Klein • Franklin Square, NY

caramel pecan pie

PREP: 25 MIN. BAKE: 35 MIN. + COOLING

This is hands down the best pecan pie.
Dorothy Reinhold • Malibu, CA

- 36 caramels
- 1/4 cup water
- 1/4 cup butter, cubed
- 3 eggs
- 3/4 cup sugar
- 1 teaspoon vanilla extract
- 1/8 teaspoon salt
- 1-1/3 cups chopped pecans, toasted
- 1 unbaked deep-dish pastry shell (9 inches)
- Pecan halves, optional

1 In a small heavy saucepan, combine the caramels, water and butter. Cook and stir over low heat until caramels are melted. Remove from the heat and set aside.

2 In a small bowl, beat the eggs, sugar, vanilla and salt until smooth. Gradually add caramel mixture. Stir in chopped pecans. Pour into pastry shell. If desired, arrange pecan halves over filling.

3 Bake at 350° for 35-40 minutes or until set. Cool on a wire rack. Refrigerate leftovers.

YIELD: 6-8 SERVINGS.

Several years ago, a coworker came across candies like these in a store and asked if I could make them. After some trial and error, I came up with a winning recipe.

Karen Daniels
Jefferson City, MO

caramel cashew clusters

PREP: 25 MIN. + STANDING

2 pounds milk chocolate candy coating, coarsely chopped, divided

1 cup salted cashew halves

28 caramels

2 tablespoons heavy whipping cream

1 Line baking sheets with waxed paper and butter the paper; set aside. In a microwave, melt 1 pound of candy coating; stir until smooth. Drop by scant tablespoonfuls onto prepared pans. Let stand until partially set, about 3 minutes. Top each with six or seven cashews. Let stand until completely set.

2 In a small heavy saucepan, combine caramels and cream. Cook and stir over low heat until melted; stir until smooth. Spoon over cashews. Reheat caramel over low heat if it thickens. Melt remaining candy coating; spoon over caramel. Let stand until set.

YIELD: 2-1/2 DOZEN.

chocolate hazelnut parfaits

PREP: 10 MIN. + CHILLING

3 cups cold milk

1 cup refrigerated hazelnut nondairy creamer

2 packages (3.9 ounces each) instant chocolate pudding mix

1 cup crushed shortbread cookies

2 cups sliced fresh strawberries

Whipped cream, optional

1 In a large bowl, whisk the milk, creamer and pudding mixes for 2 minutes. Let stand for 2 minutes or until soft-set.

2 Spoon 1/4 cup pudding into each of eight parfait glasses; sprinkle each with 1 tablespoon cookie crumbs. Top with strawberries and remaining pudding and crumbs. Refrigerate for 1 hour before serving. Garnish with whipped cream if desired.

YIELD: 8 SERVINGS.

chocolate cheesecake phyllo tartlets

PREP/TOTAL TIME: 15 MIN.

A crisp phyllo shell holds a mousse-like filling in this festive treat. The bite-size portion is perfect for parties.

Giovanna Kranenberg • Cambridge, MN

- 1 package (8 ounces) cream cheese, softened
- 1/4 cup sugar
- 1/4 cup semisweet chocolate chips, melted
- 1/2 teaspoon vanilla extract
- 2 packages (1.9 ounces each) frozen miniature phyllo tart shells
- Chocolate curls, optional

1 In a small bowl, beat the cream cheese, sugar, melted chocolate and vanilla until smooth.

2 Cut a small hole in the corner of a pastry or plastic bag and insert #32 star pastry tip. Fill the bag with the cream cheese mixture; pipe into tart shells. Garnish with the chocolate curls if desired. Refrigerate until serving.

YIELD: 2-1/2 DOZEN.

Make a quick treat by mixing dried tropical fruits with melted white chocolate.

Taste of Home Test Kitchen

chocolate curls

Use a veggie peeler to "peel" curls from a solid block of chocolate. To keep strips intact, allow them to fall gently onto a plate or waxed paper. If you get only shavings, your chocolate may be too hard, so warm it slightly.

fruit drop candies

PREP: 10 MIN. + CHILLING

- 12 ounces white baking chocolate, chopped
- 1 package (8 ounces) mixed dried fruit
- 1/2 cup chopped slivered almonds

1 In a microwave-safe bowl, melt the white chocolate; stir until smooth. Stir in the fruit and almonds until well coated.

2 Drop by tablespoonfuls into 16 mounds onto a waxed paper-lined pan. Chill until set.

YIELD: 16 PIECES.

puttin'-on-the-ritz candy

PREP: 45 MIN. + CHILLING

1 jar (12-1/4 ounces) caramel ice cream topping
1 cup chopped pecans
36 butter-flavored crackers
1 cup (6 ounces) semisweet chocolate chips
1 tablespoon shortening

1 In a microwave-safe bowl, heat the caramel topping and pecans on high for 5-7 minutes, stirring frequently until mixture is thickened. Cool for 5 minutes. Place the crackers on waxed paper-lined baking sheets. Spoon 1 teaspoon caramel mixture over each cracker. Refrigerate for 1 hour.

2 In a microwave, melt chocolate chips and shortening; stir until smooth. Dip the bottom of each cracker in chocolate; shake off excess. Place caramel side down on waxed paper-lined pans. Refrigerate for 1 hour or until set. Store in an airtight container.

YIELD: 3 DOZEN.

dipped spice cookies

PREP: 25 MIN. • BAKE: 10 MIN./BATCH + STANDING

- 1/2 tube refrigerated sugar cookie dough, softened
- 1/2 cup all-purpose flour
- 1/4 cup packed brown sugar
- 1 tablespoon orange juice
- 3/4 teaspoon ground cinnamon
- 1/2 teaspoon ground ginger
- 1/2 teaspoon grated orange peel
- 1/2 cup semisweet chocolate chips
- 4 teaspoons shortening
- 1/4 cup finely chopped walnuts

1 In a large bowl, beat the cookie dough, flour, brown sugar, orange juice, cinnamon, ginger and orange peel until combined. Shape teaspoonfuls of dough into 2-in. logs. Place 2 in. apart on ungreased baking sheets.

2 Bake at 350° for 8-10 minutes or until edges are golden brown. Remove to wire racks to cool.

3 In a microwave-safe bowl, melt chocolate chips and shortening; stir until smooth. Dip one end of each cookie into melted chocolate, allowing excess to drip off; sprinkle with walnuts. Place on waxed paper; let stand until set.

YIELD: ABOUT 3-1/2 DOZEN.

A hint of orange and a sprinkling of spices lend old-fashioned goodness to these delightful treats. The logs are dipped in melted chocolate and sprinkled with nuts for extra appeal.
Taste of Home Test Kitchen

cream cheese cookie cups

PREP: 15 MIN. • BAKE: 10 MIN. + COOLING

Need a quick dessert? Try these yummy cookie bites. For a pretty look, use an icing bag to pipe the filling into the cups, then top each with mini M&M's.

Rachel Blackston • Mauk, GA

- 1 tube (18 ounces) refrigerated chocolate chip cookie dough
- 4 ounces cream cheese, softened
- 2 tablespoons butter, softened
- 1/2 teaspoon vanilla extract
- 1-1/4 cups confectioners' sugar

1 Cut cookie dough in half (save one portion for another use). With floured hands, press about 1 tablespoon of dough onto the bottom and up the sides of 12 ungreased miniature muffin cups. Bake at 350° for 8-10 minutes or until lightly browned.

2 Using the end of a wooden spoon handle, reshape the puffed cookie cups. Cool for 5 minutes before removing from pan to a wire rack to cool completely.

3 In a small bowl, beat the cream cheese, butter and vanilla until smooth. Gradually beat in confectioners' sugar. Spoon into cookie cups. Store in the refrigerator.

YIELD: 1 DOZEN.

praline-peach brownie sundaes

PREP/TOTAL TIME: 20 MIN.

1/4 cup packed brown sugar

1/4 cup heavy whipping cream

2 tablespoons butter

1/4 teaspoon ground cinnamon

2 medium peaches, peeled and sliced or 1 cup frozen unsweetened peach slices, thawed and patted dry

1/2 cup chopped pecans

1 teaspoon vanilla extract

6 prepared brownies

3 cups vanilla ice cream

Additional peach slices, optional

1 In a large saucepan, whisk the brown sugar, cream, butter and cinnamon until smooth. Bring to a boil; cook and stir for 6-7 minutes or until thickened. Remove from the heat; stir in the peaches, pecans and vanilla. Cool for 10 minutes.

2 Place brownies in dessert dishes; top with ice cream and peach sauce. Garnish with additional peach slices if desired.

YIELD: 6 SERVINGS.

Raspberry pie filling and homemade chocolate frosting jazz up a packaged cake mix in this picture-perfect torte. With a hint of rum flavor, it's rich and creamy for special occasions but so simple to do, you could prepare it on weeknights, too.

Taste of Home
Test Kitchen

raspberry butter torte

PREP: 30 MIN. • BAKE: 30 MIN. + COOLING

1 package (18-1/2 ounces) butter recipe golden cake mix
1/4 cup chopped almonds, toasted
2 cups heavy whipping cream
1 cup confectioners' sugar
1/4 cup baking cocoa
1-1/2 teaspoons rum extract
2 cups raspberry filling
Chocolate curls
Sliced almonds, toasted, optional

1 Prepare cake batter according to package directions; fold in chopped almonds. Pour into two greased and floured 9-in. round baking pans. Bake as directed. Cool for 10 minutes before removing from pans to wire racks to cool completely.

2 For frosting, in a small bowl, beat cream until it begins to thicken. Add the confectioners' sugar, cocoa and extract; beat until stiff peaks form.

3 Cut each cake into two horizontal layers. Place one layer on a serving plate; spread with 1/2 cup raspberry filling and 1/2 cup frosting. Repeat with remaining cake layers.

4 Place remaining frosting in a pastry bag with a star tip #195. Decorate top and sides of cake as desired. Garnish with chocolate curls. Sprinkle with sliced almonds if desired. Store in the refrigerator.

YIELD: 12-14 SERVINGS.

EDITOR'S NOTE: For the cake pictured, pipe about 1/2 cup frosting around the cake between layers and 1-1/2 cups on top.

chewy caramel bars

PREP: 10 MIN. • BAKE: 40 MIN. + COOLING

- 1 package (18-1/4 ounces) yellow cake mix
- 1 can (5 ounces) evaporated milk
- 1/4 cup butter, melted
- 1/2 cup chopped nuts
- 36 Rolo candies, halved

1. In a large bowl, beat the cake mix, milk and butter until blended (batter will be thick). Stir in nuts. Press half of mixture into a 13-in. x 9-in. baking pan coated with cooking spray. Bake at 350° for 10-12 minutes or until set.

2. Place candies, cut side down, over crust. Drop remaining batter by tablespoonfuls over the top. Bake 25-30 minutes longer or until golden brown. Cool on a wire rack. Cut into bars.

YIELD: 2 DOZEN.

grasshopper pie

PREP: 15 MIN. + CHILLING

This pie has been a longtime Christmas classic in our family, but it's so delicious, I now make it throughout the year!

Melissa Sokasits • Warrenville, IL

- 1-1/2 cups cold milk
- 1 package (3.9 ounces) instant chocolate pudding mix
- 2-3/4 cups whipped topping, divided
- 1 package (4.67 ounces) mint Andes candies, chopped, divided
- 1 chocolate crumb crust (9 inches)
- 1/4 teaspoon mint extract
- 2 drops green food coloring, optional

1. In a small bowl, whisk milk and pudding mix for 2 minutes. Let stand for 2 minutes or until soft-set. Fold in 3/4 cup whipped topping. Fold in 3/4 cup candies. Spoon into crust.

2. In another bowl, combine the extract and the remaining whipped topping; add food coloring if desired. Spread over pudding layer; sprinkle with remaining candies. Cover and refrigerate for 4 hours or until set.

YIELD: 8 SERVINGS.

This sweet and salty pie is often requested by my family at get-togethers. Serve with vanilla ice cream for extra decadence.

Dulcie Knoll
Bluffton, SC

caramel nut pie

PREP: 15 MIN. • BAKE: 30 MIN. + CHILLING

3 eggs

3/4 cup Milky Way ice cream topping

1/2 cup sugar

1/4 cup light corn syrup

2 tablespoons butter, melted

1 teaspoon vanilla extract

1/8 teaspoon salt

1 unbaked pastry shell (9 inches)

1 cup chopped unsalted dry roasted peanuts

1/2 cup chopped walnuts

1 In a small bowl, whisk the eggs, ice cream topping, sugar, corn syrup, butter, vanilla and salt until blended. Pour into pastry shell; sprinkle with nuts. Cover edges with foil.

2 Bake at 400° for 10 minutes. Reduce heat to 350°; bake 20-25 minutes longer or until filling is almost set. Cool on a wire rack. Refrigerate for 1-2 hours before serving.

YIELD: 6-8 SERVINGS.

black forest cheesecake

PREP: 20 MIN. + CHILLING

1 package (8 ounces) cream cheese, softened

1/3 cup sugar

1 cup (8 ounces) sour cream

2 teaspoons vanilla extract

1 carton (8 ounces) frozen whipped topping, thawed

1 chocolate crumb crust (8 inches)

1/4 cup baking cocoa

1 tablespoon confectioners' sugar

1 can (21 ounces) cherry pie filling

1 In a large bowl, beat cream cheese and sugar until smooth. Beat in sour cream and vanilla. Fold in whipped topping. Spread half of the mixture evenly into crust. Fold cocoa and confectioners' sugar into remaining whipped topping mixture; carefully spread over cream cheese layer. Refrigerate for at least 4 hours.

2 Cut into slices; top each slice with cherry pie filling. Refrigerate leftovers.

YIELD: 6-8 SERVINGS.

These yummy mint chocolate bites are so delightful, you'll find it difficult to stop at one. With a combination of sweetness and crunch from the chocolate cookies, they make pretty holiday gifts with candy canes or other candies on top.

Taste of Home
Test Kitchen

mint cookie candies

PREP/TOTAL TIME: 30 MIN.

12 ounces white candy coating, coarsely chopped

6 teaspoons shortening, divided

1/4 teaspoon green food coloring

4 mint cream-filled chocolate sandwich cookies, crushed

2 packages (4.67 ounces each) mint Andes candies

1 In a microwave-safe bowl, melt candy coating and 4 teaspoons shortening; stir until smooth. Stir in food coloring. Pour evenly into miniature muffin cup liners. Sprinkle with cookie crumbs.

2 In a microwave, melt mint candies and remaining shortening; stir until smooth. Pour over cookie crumbs. Let stand until set.

YIELD: 4 DOZEN.

With the flavor of vanilla chips and a creamy filling, this luscious cheesecake-like dessert is a cinch to prepare. Sometimes I garnish with shaved chocolate to dress it up.

Melanie Budd
Anaconda, MT

vanilla chip dessert

PREP: 30 MIN. + CHILLING

3 cups crushed vanilla wafers (about 90 wafers)

1/2 cup butter, melted

3 tablespoons brown sugar

1 package (10 to 12 ounces) white baking chips

2 packages (8 ounces each) cream cheese, softened

2 cups (16 ounces) sour cream

1 carton (8 ounces) frozen whipped topping, thawed

Chocolate ice cream topping, optional

1 In a large bowl, combine the wafer crumbs, butter and brown sugar. Press onto the bottom of a greased 13-in. x 9-in. baking dish. Bake at 350° for 5-8 minutes or until lightly browned. Cool.

2 In a microwave, melt the white chips and stir until smooth. Cool.

3 In a large bowl, beat cream cheese and sour cream until smooth. Add melted chips; beat well. Fold in whipped topping.

4 Pour filling over crust. Cover and refrigerate for 2 hours or until set. Drizzle with the chocolate topping if desired.

YIELD: 15 SERVINGS.

coconut strawberry phyllo cones

PREP: 35 MIN. • BAKE: 5 MIN. + COOLING

4 sheets phyllo dough (14 inches x 9 inches)
1 cup cold fat-free milk
1/2 teaspoon coconut extract
1 package (3.4 ounces) instant vanilla pudding mix
1/3 cup flaked coconut, finely chopped
1/2 cup reduced-fat whipped topping
6 fresh strawberries, divided

1 Cut four 12-in. x 6-in. pieces of foil. Fold each in half widthwise. Shape each square into a loosely rolled cone, overlapping the edges about 1-1/2 in.; set aside.

2 Place one sheet of phyllo dough on a work surface; spray with cooking spray. Repeat with one more sheet of phyllo. Keep remaining phyllo covered with plastic wrap and a damp towel to prevent drying out. Cut in half lengthwise and widthwise. Carefully wrap one phyllo section around each foil cone; spray again with cooking spray.

3 Place on an ungreased baking sheet. Bake at 425° for 4-5 minutes or until lightly browned. Immediately remove phyllo from foil cones to a wire rack to cool completely. Repeat entire procedure with remaining phyllo dough.

4 In a small bowl, whisk the milk, extract and pudding for 2 minutes; fold in coconut and whipped topping. Spoon into a pastry bag fitted with a star tip. Finely chop three strawberries and spoon inside the cones. Pipe pudding mixture into cones. Slice remaining strawberries to use as garnish. Serve immediately.

YIELD: 8 SERVINGS.

rice pudding tartlets

PREP/TOTAL TIME: 25 MIN.

10 large marshmallows
1 tablespoon butter
1-1/2 cups crisp rice cereal
1/4 cup flaked coconut
1 carton (16 ounces) prepared rice pudding
1 tablespoon cold milk
1/2 cup golden raisins
Ground cinnamon, optional

1 In a large microwave-safe bowl, microwave the marshmallows and butter until melted; stir until smooth. Stir in the cereal and coconut until combined.

2 Coat six 6-oz. custard cups with cooking spray; press 1/4 cup cereal mixture onto the bottom and up the sides of each cup. Let stand for 15 minutes.

3 In a large bowl, combine the pudding, milk and raisins. Remove the cereal cups from the custard cups; fill with pudding mixture. Sprinkle with cinnamon if desired.

YIELD: 6 SERVINGS.

strawberry banana squares

PREP: 15 MIN. • BAKE: 40 MIN. + COOLING

The combined flavors of strawberry, banana and coconut create a winning recipe. This dessert really does have it all, and your kids will notice!

Lucille Mead • Ilion, NY

- 1 package (14 ounces) banana quick bread and muffin mix
- 1/2 cup chopped walnuts
- 1/3 cup butter, softened
- 1 egg
- 1 can (14 ounces) sweetened condensed milk
- 1 can (20 ounces) strawberry pie filling
- 1/2 cup flaked coconut

1 In a small bowl, combine the bread mix, walnuts, butter and egg until crumbly. Press onto the bottom of a 13-in. x 9-in. baking dish coated with cooking spray. Bake at 350° for 8-10 minutes or until lightly browned.

2 Spread the milk over crust; spoon pie filling over milk. Sprinkle with coconut. Bake 30-40 minutes longer or until golden brown. Cool on a wire rack. Cut into squares.

YIELD: 2 DOZEN.

For dessert on the double, luscious Snickerdoodle Sundaes can't be beat. I whip up the easy caramel-topped recipe with my two daughters. It is so simple (but special enough) to fix for guests. And it always brings raves.

Melissa Van Bramer • Pickerington, OH

cutting bars

For perfectly sized bars, lay a clean ruler on top of the bars and make cut marks with the point of a knife. Use the edge of the ruler as a cutting guide.

snickerdoodle sundaes

PREP/TOTAL TIME: 30 MIN.

- 1 package (17-1/2 ounces) sugar cookie mix
- 2 cups cinnamon ice cream or ice cream of your choice
- 1/2 cup caramel ice cream topping

1 Prepare and bake cookies according to package directions. Set aside 8 cookies (save remaining cookies for another use). Place 2 cookies in each serving bowl. Top with 1/2 cup ice cream; drizzle with 2 tablespoons caramel topping.

YIELD: 4 SERVINGS.

I use time-saving apple pie filling and a convenient pastry shell crust for this scrumptious pie. Dressed up with a crunchy streusel topping, it is a sweet afternoon pick-me-up or dinnertime finale.

Billie Moss
Walnut Creek, CA

peanut butter crumb apple pie

PREP: 10 MIN. • BAKE: 20 MIN. + COOLING

1 can (21 ounces) apple pie filling
1 teaspoon lemon juice
1 pastry shell (9 inches), baked
1/2 cup all-purpose flour
1/3 cup packed brown sugar
1 to 3 teaspoons grated lemon peel
1/2 teaspoon ground cinnamon
1/4 teaspoon ground nutmeg
6 tablespoons chunky peanut butter
2 tablespoons cold butter

1 In a small bowl, combine the pie filling and lemon juice; spoon into pastry shell.

2 In a large bowl, combine the flour, brown sugar, lemon peel, cinnamon and nutmeg; cut in peanut butter and butter until crumbly. Sprinkle over filling.

3 Bake at 400° for 20-22 minutes or until topping is lightly browned. Cool on a wire rack.

YIELD: 6-8 SERVINGS.

blueberry fluff pie

PREP: 25 MIN. + CHILLING

This light dessert is a perfect ending to any meal. The original recipe from Mom called for sliced peaches, which are also good. I have used fresh raspberries, too.

Shirley Dierold • Stroudsburg, PA

20 large marshmallows
1/4 cup milk
4 cups fresh blueberries, divided
1 carton (8 ounces) frozen whipped topping, thawed
1 pastry shell (9 inches), baked

1 In a heavy saucepan, combine marshmallows and milk. Cook and stir over medium-low heat until marshmallows are melted and mixture is smooth. Cool for 8-10 minutes, stirring several times.

2 Stir in 3-1/2 cups blueberries. Set aside 1/2 cup whipped topping; fold remaining topping into blueberry mixture. Pour into crust. Refrigerate for at least 2 hours. Garnish with remaining blueberries and reserved topping.

YIELD: 8 SERVINGS.

Add apples and a crumb topping to packaged gingerbread cake mix for a speedy treat that's sure to become a family favorite in your household.

Taste of Home
Test Kitchen

apple gingerbread cake

PREP: 5 MIN. • BAKE: 25 MIN. + COOLING

1 package (14-1/2 ounces) gingerbread cake/cookie mix

1-1/4 cups water

1 egg

1 cup chopped peeled apple

1/2 cup chopped pecans

2 tablespoons brown sugar

1 In a large bowl, beat the cake mix, water and egg until combined. Add apple; stir to combine. Transfer to a greased 11-in. x 7-in. baking dish. Combine the pecans and brown sugar; sprinkle over the top.

2 Bake at 350° for 23-25 minutes or until a toothpick inserted near the center comes out clean. Cool on a wire rack.

YIELD: 9 SERVINGS.

chocolate chip cookie pizza

PREP: 25 MIN. • BAKE: 15 MIN. + COOLING

- 1 tube (16-1/2 ounces) refrigerated chocolate chip cookie dough
- 1 package (8 ounces) cream cheese, softened
- 1/3 cup sugar
- 2 cups cold half-and-half cream
- 1 package (3.9 ounces) instant chocolate pudding mix
- 1/4 cup chopped pecans or walnuts

1 Press cookie dough onto an ungreased 12-in. pizza pan. Bake at 350° for 15-20 minutes or until deep golden brown. Cool for 5 minutes; gently run a flexible metal spatula under crust to loosen. Cool completely.

2 In a small bowl, beat the cream cheese and sugar until blended. Spread over crust. In a large bowl, whisk cream and pudding mix for 2 minutes. Let stand for 2 minutes or until soft-set. Spread over the cream cheese mixture; sprinkle with nuts. Refrigerate until serving.

YIELD: 14-16 SLICES.

cream cheese

To soften cream cheese, cut it into small cubes and let stand at room temperature until soft. Or place, unwrapped, on a micro-wave-safe plate and microwave at 50% power for 10-second intervals until softened.

The tart cranberries in this pie dress up sweet canned cherry pie filling. You can serve this dessert during the summer or as a unique treat during the holiday season.

Rita Krajcir
West Allis, WI

cranberry cherry pie

PREP: 20 MIN. • BAKE: 40 MIN.

Pastry for double-crust pie (9 inches)
2 cups fresh or frozen cranberries, thawed
3/4 cup plus 2 teaspoons sugar, divided
2 tablespoons cornstarch
1 can (21 ounces) cherry pie filling
1 egg white
1 teaspoon water

1 Line a 9-in. pie plate with bottom pastry; trim even with the edge of plate. Set aside. In a large bowl, combine the cranberries, 3/4 cup sugar and cornstarch; stir in cherry pie filling. Spoon into crust.

2 Roll out remaining pastry; make a lattice crust. Trim, seal and flute edges. Whisk together egg white and water; brush over crust. Sprinkle with the remaining sugar.

3 Cover the edges loosely with foil. Bake at 425° for 25 minutes. Remove foil; bake 15-20 minutes longer or until crust is golden brown and filling is bubbly. Cool on a wire rack.

YIELD: 6-8 SERVINGS.

pudding pound cake dessert

PREP/TOTAL TIME: 30 MIN.

- 1 frozen pound cake (10-3/4 ounces), thawed
- 3 cups cold milk
- 2 packages (3.9 ounces each) instant chocolate pudding mix
- 3 cups whipped topping
- 1/2 cup chopped walnuts
- 3/4 cup chopped cream-filled chocolate sandwich cookies

1 Cut cake horizontally into fourths; place two pieces side by side in an 8-in. square dish. In a large bowl, whisk milk and pudding mixes for 2 minutes. Let stand for 2 minutes or until soft-set; fold in the whipped topping.

2 Spoon half over cake; sprinkle with walnuts and 1/2 cup cookies. Layer with remaining cake, pudding mixture and cookies (dish will be full). Refrigerate until serving.

YIELD: 9 SERVINGS.

raspberry brownie dessert

PREP: 20 MIN. • BAKE: 25 MIN. + CHILLING

This is such an easy dessert to make that everyone goes crazy over it! I have brought it to church and office potlucks, and everyone always begs for more.

Ann Vick • Rosemount, MN

- 1 package fudge brownie mix (13-inch x 9-inch pan size)
- 2 cups heavy whipping cream, divided
- 1 package (3.3 ounces) instant white chocolate pudding mix
- 1 can (21 ounces) raspberry pie filling

1 Prepare and bake brownies according to package directions, using a greased 13-in. x 9-in. baking pan. Cool completely on a wire rack.

2 In a small bowl, combine 1 cup cream and pudding mix; stir for 2 minutes or until very thick. In a small bowl, beat remaining cream until stiff peaks form; fold into pudding. Carefully spread over brownies; top with pie filling. Cover and refrigerate for at least 2 hours before cutting.

YIELD: 15-18 SERVINGS.

This four-ingredient dessert can be ready in 10 minutes. When fresh peaches are not available, simply use frozen sliced peaches and adjust the microwave time.

Taste of Home Test Kitchen

freezing tips

Most bars and brownies freeze well for up to 3 months. To freeze a pan of uncut bars, place in an airtight container or resealable plastic bag. Thaw at room temperature before serving.

peaches 'n' cream crisp

PREP/TOTAL TIME: 10 MIN.

- 3 cups fresh or frozen sliced peaches
- 4 teaspoons butterscotch ice cream topping
- 4 tablespoons granola cereal without raisins
- 4 scoops vanilla ice cream

1 Place the peaches in four 8-oz. ramekins or custard cups. Top with butterscotch topping and granola. Microwave, uncovered, on high for 2-3 minutes or until bubbly. Top with ice cream.

YIELD: 4 SERVINGS.

cake & berry campfire delight

PREP: 10 MIN. • GRILL: 30 MIN.

2 cans (21 ounces each) raspberry pie filling
1 package (18-1/4 ounces) yellow cake mix
1-1/4 cups water
1/2 cup canola oil
Vanilla ice cream, optional

1 Prepare grill or campfire for low heat, using 16-20 charcoal briquettes or large wood chips.

2 Line a Dutch oven with heavy-duty aluminum foil; add pie filling. In a large bowl, combine the cake mix, water and oil. Spread over pie filling.

3 Cover Dutch oven. When briquettes or wood chips are covered with white ash, place Dutch oven directly on top of 8-10 of them. Using long-handled tongs, place remaining briquettes on pan cover.

4 Cook for 30-40 minutes or until the filling is bubbly and a toothpick inserted in the topping comes out clean. To check for doneness, use tongs to carefully lift the cover. Serve with ice cream if desired.

YIELD: 12 SERVINGS.

EDITOR'S NOTE: This recipe does not use eggs.

Pomegranate seeds add a nice touch to this tropical fruit topping. To seed a pomegranate, cut off the crown, score into quarters and soak in a large bowl of cold water for 5 minutes. Holding underwater, break the scored sections apart with your fingers. Separate the seed clusters from the skin and membranes. Discard the skin and the membranes; dry the seeds on paper towels.

Taste of Home
Test Kitchen

tropical pound cake

PREP/TOTAL TIME: 15 MIN.

4 tablespoons butter, divided

1 package (10-3/4 ounces) frozen pound cake, thawed and cut into 12 slices

2 cans (15-1/4 ounces each) mixed tropical fruit, drained

2 tablespoons honey

6 tablespoons flaked coconut, toasted

Pomegranate seeds, optional

1 Melt 2 tablespoons butter; lightly brush over one side of each cake slice. Place buttered side up in a foil-lined 15-in. x 10-in. x 1-in. pan. Broil 3-4 in. from the heat for 1-2 minutes or until golden brown.

2 In a large skillet, melt remaining butter; add fruit. Cook and stir over medium heat for 5 minutes or until heated through. Stir in honey; cook for 2 minutes.

3 Place two cake slices on each of six dessert plates. Top each with 1/2 cup fruit mixture and sprinkle with coconut. Garnish desserts with pomegranate seeds if desired.

YIELD: 6 SERVINGS.

Whether celebrating the holidays or hosting a casual get-together, creating fun and fabulous food is a cinch with these fast-to-fix recipes.

holidays & parties

Valentine's Day doesn't get much sweeter than when this fudge-covered creation makes an appearance. The berry-topped masterpiece starts with a cake mix, so preparation is a snap.

Taste of Home
Test Kitchen

devilish valentine's cake

PREP: 10 MIN. • BAKE: 25 MIN.

1 package (9 ounces) devil's food cake mix
3/4 cup semisweet chocolate chunks
1/2 cup hot fudge ice cream topping
1-1/2 cups fresh raspberries

1 Grease a 9-in. heart-shaped baking pan. Line with waxed paper; grease and flour the paper. Set aside. Prepare cake batter according to package directions; stir in chocolate chunks. Pour into prepared pan.

2 Bake at 350° for 25-30 minutes or until a toothpick inserted near the center comes out clean. Cool for 5 minutes before inverting onto a serving platter. Spread warm cake with hot fudge topping. Arrange raspberries over the top.

YIELD: 6-8 SERVINGS.

For dessert, present this sweet-tart combination of cherry pie filling and fresh cranberries. Individual servings of the warm fruit mixture are garnished with pretty pastry crust hearts.

Taste of Home
Test Kitchen

sweetheart dessert

PREP/TOTAL TIME: 25 MIN.

1/2 cup plus 1 tablespoon sugar, divided

1 tablespoon cornstarch

1 can (21 ounces) cherry pie filling

1 cup fresh or frozen cranberries, coarsely chopped

1 sheet refrigerated pie pastry

1/4 teaspoon ground cinnamon

1 In a large bowl, combine 1/2 cup sugar and cornstarch. Stir in the pie filling and cranberries. Spoon into four ungreased 6-oz. baking dishes. Bake at 425° for 15-20 minutes or until thickened and bubbly.

2 Meanwhile, cut eight hearts from pastry with a 2-1/2-in. heart-shaped cookie cutter. Place on an ungreased baking sheet. Combine cinnamon and remaining sugar; sprinkle over hearts. Bake for 8-11 minutes or until edges are lightly browned. Place two hearts on each dessert. Serve warm.

YIELD: 4 SERVINGS.

peeps sunflower cake

PREP: 15 MIN. • BAKE: 30 MIN. + COOLING

1 package (18-1/4 ounces) yellow cake mix
2 cans (16 ounces each) chocolate frosting
19 yellow chick Peeps candies
1-1/2 cups semisweet chocolate chips

1 Prepare and bake cake according to package directions, using two greased and waxed paper-lined 9-in. round baking pans. Cool for 10 minutes before removing from pans to wire racks to cool completely; carefully remove waxed paper.

2 Level tops of cakes. Spread frosting between layers and over the top and sides of cake.

3 Without separating Peeps and curving slightly to fit, arrange chicks around edge of cake for sunflower petals. For sunflower seeds, arrange chocolate chips in center of cake.

YIELD: 12 SERVINGS.

nesting chicks

PREP/TOTAL TIME: 30 MIN.

- 1 package (10-1/2 ounces) miniature marshmallows
- 2 tablespoons butter
- 1 teaspoon water
- 4 drops green food coloring
- 1-1/2 cups flaked coconut
- 6 cups Corn Pops
- 1/2 cup jelly beans
- 16 Peeps

1 In a large saucepan, combine marshmallows and butter. Cook and stir over low heat until melted and smooth. Meanwhile, in a small resealable plastic bag, combine water and food coloring. Add coconut; seal bag and shake to tint. Set aside.

2 Place the cereal in a large bowl; add marshmallow mixture and stir until combined. Press into greased muffin cups. Let stand until serving. Remove nests from the cups; top with tinted coconut, jelly beans and Peeps.

YIELD: 16 SERVINGS.

Finish off a summer meal with the fresh-squeezed flavor of this pretty pie. Guests will love the tangy, light and refreshing finale to dinner and never guess how simple it is to prepare. For added convenience, make it ahead of time and tuck it in the fridge!

Taste of Home Test Kitchen

poppy seed lemon pie

PREP/TOTAL TIME: 10 MIN.

1 can (14 ounces) sweetened condensed milk
1/3 cup thawed lemonade concentrate
1 carton (8 ounces) frozen whipped topping, thawed, divided
1 graham cracker crust (9 inches)
1 tablespoon poppy seeds
10 to 12 drops yellow food coloring, optional

1 In a large bowl, beat milk and lemonade concentrate until smooth (mixture will begin to thicken). Fold in 2 cups whipped topping. Spread half into the crust.

2 Add poppy seeds and food coloring if desired to the remaining lemon mixture; stir until blended. Spoon over first layer. Spread with the remaining whipped topping. Refrigerate until serving.

YIELD: 6-8 SERVINGS.

holiday pistachio dessert

PREP: 30 MIN. + CHILLING

1-1/4 cups biscuit/baking mix

1/2 cup chopped walnuts

1 tablespoon brown sugar

3 tablespoons cold butter

1 package (8 ounces) cream cheese, softened

1 cup plus 1 tablespoon confectioners' sugar, divided

1 cup heavy whipping cream, whipped, divided

2-1/2 cups cold milk

2 packages (3.4 ounces each) instant pistachio pudding mix

Chocolate curls, optional

1 In a small bowl, combine the biscuit mix, walnuts and brown sugar. Cut in butter until mixture resembles coarse crumbs.

2 Press into an ungreased 13-in. x 9-in. baking pan. Bake at 375° for 10-12 minutes or until lightly browned. Cool on a wire rack.

3 In a small bowl, beat cream cheese and 1 cup confectioners' sugar until fluffy. Fold in half of the whipped cream; spread over crust. Stir remaining confectioners' sugar into remaining whipped cream; refrigerate until serving.

4 In another bowl, whisk milk and pudding mixes for 2 minutes. Let stand for 2 minutes or until soft-set. Spread over cream cheese layer. Cover and refrigerate for at least 4 hours before serving.

5 Garnish with sweetened whipped cream and chocolate curls if desired.

YIELD: 15 SERVINGS.

Filled with a scrumptious, packaged rice mixture and seasoned with teriyaki sauce, these steaks are a favorite for company. Just four ingredients are required for the delightful entree, so it comes together in a snap.

Ardith Baker
Beaverton, OR

wild rice-stuffed steaks

PREP/TOTAL TIME: 30 MIN.

1 package (6.2 ounces) fast-cooking long grain and wild rice mix

1/4 cup chopped green onions

6 boneless beef top loin steaks (12 ounces each)

1/2 cup teriyaki sauce, divided

1 Cook the rice according to package directions for microwave; cool. Stir in the onions. Cut a pocket in each steak by slicing to within 1/2 in. of bottom. Stuff each with 1/4 cup rice mixture; secure with toothpicks. Brush the steaks with 2 tablespoons teriyaki sauce.

2 Place on a broiler pan. Broil 4-6 in. from heat for 4-6 minutes. Turn steaks; brush with 2 tablespoons teriyaki sauce. Broil 6-8 minutes longer or until meat reaches desired doneness (for medium-rare, a meat thermometer should read 145°; medium, 160°; well-done, 170°), basting frequently with remaining sauce. Discard toothpicks.

YIELD: 6 SERVINGS.

EDITOR'S NOTE: Top loin steak may be labeled as strip steak, Kansas City steak, New York strip steak, ambassador steak or boneless club steak in your region.

stuffed butterflied shrimp

PREP: 20 MIN. + STANDING • BAKE: 20 MIN.

24 uncooked unpeeled large shrimp

1 cup Italian salad dressing

1-1/2 cups seasoned bread crumbs

1 can (6-1/2 ounces) chopped clams, drained and minced

6 tablespoons butter, melted

1-1/2 teaspoons minced fresh parsley

1 Peel shrimp, leaving tail section on. Make a deep cut along the top of each shrimp (do not cut all the way through); remove the vein. Place shrimp in a shallow dish; add salad dressing. Set aside for 20 minutes.

2 Meanwhile, in a large bowl, combine the bread crumbs, clams, butter and parsley. Drain and discard salad dressing. Arrange shrimp in a greased 13-in. x 9-in. baking dish. Open shrimp and press flat; fill each with 1 tablespoon of crumb mixture. Bake, uncovered, at 350° for 20-25 minutes or until shrimp turn pink.

YIELD: 2 DOZEN.

My flavorful baked shrimp can be an appetizer or entree. I've handed out this recipe to many friends and family.
Joan Elliott • Deep River, CT

wearing o' green cake

PREP: 25 MIN. • BAKE: 30 MIN. + COOLING

One bite of this moist, colorful cake and you'll think you've found the pot o' gold at the end of the rainbow. It's the perfect dessert to round out your St. Patrick's Day feast!
Marge Nicol • Shannon, IL

1 package (18-1/4 ounces) white cake mix

2 packages (3 ounces each) lime gelatin

1 cup boiling water

1/2 cup cold water

TOPPING:

1 cup cold milk

1 package (3.4 ounces) instant vanilla pudding mix

1 carton (8 ounces) frozen whipped topping, thawed

Green sprinkles

1 Prepare and bake cake according to package directions, using a greased 13-in. x 9-in. baking dish. Cool on a wire rack for 1 hour. In a small bowl, dissolve gelatin in boiling water; stir in cold water and set aside.

2 With a meat fork or wooden skewer, poke holes about 2 in. apart into cooled cake. Slowly pour gelatin over cake. Cover and refrigerate.

3 In a large bowl, whisk milk and pudding mix for 2 minutes. Let stand for 2 minutes or until soft-set. Fold in whipped topping. Spread over cake. Decorate with sprinkles. Cover and refrigerate until serving.

YIELD: 12-15 SERVINGS.

star-spangled shortcake

PREP/TOTAL TIME: 30 MIN.

1 package (8-1/2 ounces) corn bread/muffin mix
2 cups halved fresh strawberries
2 cups fresh or frozen blueberries, thawed
1/3 cup sugar
5 teaspoons balsamic vinegar
Vanilla ice cream

1 Prepare corn bread batter according to package directions. Fill six greased star-shaped cups or muffin cups two-thirds full. Bake at 350° for 12-15 minutes or until a toothpick inserted near the center comes out clean.

2 Meanwhile, in a large bowl, combine the strawberries and blueberries; sprinkle with sugar and gently toss to coat.

3 Cool shortcakes for 10 minutes before carefully removing from pan to a wire rack. Drizzle vinegar over berries; toss to coat. Top each shortcake with a scoop of ice cream and berry mixture.

YIELD: 6 SERVINGS.

EDITOR'S NOTE: Star-shaped muffin pans are available from Wilton Industries, Inc. Call 800-794-5866 or visit www.wilton.com.

star-spangled fruit tart

PREP: 25 MIN. • BAKE: 10 MIN. + COOLING

- 1 tube (18 ounces) refrigerated sugar cookie dough, softened
- 1 package (8 ounces) cream cheese, softened
- 1/4 cup sugar
- 1/2 teaspoon almond extract
- 1 cup fresh blueberries
- 1 cup fresh raspberries
- 1 cup halved fresh strawberries

1 Press cookie dough onto an ungreased 12-in. pizza pan. Bake at 350° for 10-15 minutes or until golden brown. Cool on a wire rack.

2 In a small bowl, beat the cream cheese, sugar and extract until smooth. Spread over crust. In center of tart, arrange berries in the shape of a star; add a berry border. Refrigerate until serving.

YIELD: 16 SERVINGS.

My crispy, creamy dessert is perfect for a Fourth of July celebration! With patriotic colors and a light, fluffy filling, this summery delight will be the hit of your get-together.
Renae Moncur • Burley, ID

star sandwich cookies

PREP: 30 MIN. • BAKE: 10 MIN. + COOLING

These dazzling sandwich cookies are sure to be the star of your holiday dessert tray. A rich mixture of white chocolate and cream cheese forms the sweet yet simple filling.

Taste of Home Test Kitchen

- 1/2 tube refrigerated sugar cookie dough, softened
- 1/3 cup all-purpose flour
- Red sugars, nonpareils or sprinkles
- 1 ounce white baking chocolate
- 2 tablespoons cream cheese, softened
- 1 tablespoon butter, softened
- 4 drops red food coloring
- 1/2 cup confectioners' sugar

1 In a small bowl, beat the cookie dough and flour until combined. Roll out on a lightly floured surface to 1/8-in. thickness. Cut shapes with a floured 2-3/4-in. star cookie cutter. Place 2 in. apart on ungreased baking sheets.

2 Decorate half of the cookies with sugars and nonpareils. Bake at 350° for 7-9 minutes or until the edges are golden brown. Remove cookies to wire racks until cooled.

3 In a microwave, melt white chocolate; stir until smooth. Cool. In a small bowl, beat the cream cheese, butter and food coloring until fluffy. Gradually beat in confectioners' sugar and melted chocolate until smooth. Spread over the bottoms of plain cookies; top with decorated cookies. Store in the refrigerator.

YIELD: ABOUT 1 DOZEN.

baked brie with roasted garlic

PREP: 35 MIN. + COOLING • BAKE: 45 MIN.

1 whole garlic bulb

1-1/2 teaspoons plus 1 tablespoon olive oil, divided

1 tablespoon minced fresh rosemary or 1 teaspoon dried rosemary, crushed

1 round loaf (1 pound) sourdough bread

1 round (8 ounces) Brie cheese

1 loaf (10-1/2 ounces) French bread baguette, sliced and toasted

Red and green grapes

1 Remove papery outer skin from garlic (do not peel or separate cloves). Cut top off bulb. Brush with 1-1/2 teaspoons oil; sprinkle with rosemary. Wrap in heavy-duty foil. Bake at 425° for 30-35 minutes or until softened.

2 Meanwhile, cut the top fourth off the loaf of bread; carefully hollow out enough of the bottom of the bread so cheese will fit. Cube removed bread; set aside. Place cheese in bread.

3 Cool garlic for 10-15 minutes. Reduce heat to 375°. Squeeze softened garlic into a bowl and mash with a fork; spread over cheese. Replace bread top; brush outside of bread with remaining oil. Wrap in heavy-duty foil.

4 Bake for 45-50 minutes or until cheese is melted. Serve with toasted baguette, grapes and reserved bread cubes.

YIELD: 8 SERVINGS.

Looking for a standout appetizer that could double as a dessert? Try my fast, no-fuss favorite that whips up for family and friends. It's a fun change of pace for your munchies menu and an easy way to get folks to snack on apples instead of junk food.

Darlene Brenden
Salem, OR

nutty caramel
apple dip

PREP/TOTAL TIME: 15 MIN.

1 package (8 ounces) cream cheese, softened
1/2 cup apple butter
1/4 cup packed brown sugar
1/2 teaspoon vanilla extract
1/2 cup chopped salted peanuts
3 medium apples, sliced

1 In a small bowl, beat the cream cheese, apple butter, brown sugar and vanilla until combined. Stir in the peanuts. Serve with apple slices. Refrigerate leftovers.

YIELD: 2 CUPS.

EDITOR'S NOTE: This recipe was tested with commercially prepared apple butter.

spiderweb dip
with bat tortilla chips

PREP/TOTAL TIME: 30 MIN.

20 chipotle chili and pepper tortillas or flour
    tortillas (8 inches)
Cooking spray
3/4 teaspoon garlic salt
3/4 teaspoon ground coriander
3/4 teaspoon paprika
3/8 teaspoon pepper
DIP:
1 package (8 ounces) cream cheese, softened
3/4 cup salsa
1/2 cup prepared guacamole
1 to 2 tablespoons sour cream

1 Cut tortillas into bat shapes with a 3-3/4-in. cookie cutter. Place tortillas on baking sheets coated with cooking spray. Spritz tortillas with cooking spray. Combine the garlic salt, coriander, paprika and pepper; sprinkle over tortillas. Bake at 350° for 5-8 minutes or until edges just begin to brown.

2 In a small bowl, combine cream cheese and salsa. Spread into a 9-in. pie plate. Carefully spread guacamole to within 1 in. of edges.

3 Place sour cream in a small resealable plastic bag; cut a small hole in a corner of bag. Pipe thin concentric circles an inch apart over guacamole. Beginning with the center circle, gently pull a knife through circles toward outer edge. Wipe knife clean. Repeat to complete spiderweb pattern. Serve with tortilla bats.

YIELD: ABOUT 1-1/2 CUPS DIP AND ABOUT 7 DOZEN CHIPS.

mummies on a stick

PREP/TOTAL TIME: 30 MIN.

These little hot dogs are all "wrapped up" in Halloween fun. Kids really enjoy them!

Taste of Home Test Kitchen

1 tube (11 ounces) refrigerated breadsticks
10 Popsicle sticks
10 hot dogs
Prepared mustard

1 Separate dough; roll 10 pieces into 24-in. ropes. Insert a Popsicle stick into each hot dog. Starting at the stick end, wrap one dough rope around each hot dog, leaving 2 in. of the hot dog uncovered at the top for the mummy head.

2 Place mummies 1 in. apart on a greased baking sheet. Place remaining breadsticks on another baking sheet.

3 Bake at 350° for 18-20 minutes. Add dots of mustard for eyes. Save leftover breadsticks for another use.

YIELD: 10 SERVINGS.

Are these adorable or what? Little kids love to eat these colorful treats decorated with candy accents.
Taste of Home Test Kitchen

spooky punch

If you're hosting a Halloween party and want to add to the celebration with a slightly eerie beverage, try this! Combine grape and orange Kool-Aid to make a tasty black punch.

ghosts to go

PREP/TOTAL TIME: 25 MIN.

1 package (2.7 ounces) French vanilla mousse mix
3 drops each neon blue, green and purple food coloring
Assorted decorations: cake decorator hearts, red decorating gel, and purple and red Nerds

1 Prepare mousse mix according to package directions; divide into three portions. Tint one portion blue, one green and one purple.

2 Transfer each to a pastry or plastic bag; cut a hole in one corner of each bag. Pipe ghost shapes into 5-oz. plastic cups. Decorate just before serving.

YIELD: 7 SERVINGS.

There's no trick to these fun Halloween cupcakes. By using a convenient cake mix of your choice, you can turn them out in a jiffy. Simplify them even more by using canned frosting instead of making your own.

Hannah Bjerkseth
Three Hills, AB

sweet jack-o'-lanterns

PREP: 50 MIN. • BAKE: 15 MIN. + COOLING

1 package (18-1/4 ounces) yellow cake mix or cake mix of your choice

3-3/4 cups confectioners' sugar

3 tablespoons butter, softened

2/3 to 3/4 cup milk

1 to 1-1/2 teaspoons orange paste food coloring

12 gumdrops

12 black jujubes

1 Prepare and bake cake according to package directions for cupcakes. Fill 24 greased muffin cups two-thirds full. Bake at 350° for 15-18 minutes or until a toothpick inserted near the center comes out clean. Cool for 5 minutes before removing from pans to wire racks to cool completely.

2 For frosting, in a small bowl, combine confectioners' sugar, butter and enough milk to achieve spreading consistency. Stir in food coloring. Cut a thin slice off the top of each cupcake. Spread frosting on 12 cupcakes. Invert remaining cupcakes and place on top; frost top and sides.

3 For stems, place one gumdrop on each pumpkin. Cut jujubes into thin slices; use a bottom slice for each mouth.

4 From remaining slices, cut one large triangle and two smaller ones. Position two small triangles and a large triangle on each cupcake for eyes and nose.

YIELD: 1 DOZEN.

This cute cake will make your favorite trick-or-treaters smile with delight when you serve it on Halloween. The moist marble cake features a buttery frosting and fun candy pumpkins on top.

Taste of Home
Test Kitchen

halloween poke cake

PREP: 20 MIN. • BAKE: 35 MIN. + CHILLING

1 package (18-1/4 ounces) fudge marble
   cake mix
2 packages (3 ounces each) orange gelatin
1 cup boiling water
1/2 cup cold water
1/2 cup butter, softened
3-1/2 cups confectioners' sugar
1/3 cup baking cocoa
1/4 cup milk
1 teaspoon vanilla extract
12 to 15 candy pumpkins

1 Prepare and bake cake according to package directions, using a greased 13-in. x 9-in. baking pan. Cool on a wire rack for 1 hour.

2 In a small bowl, dissolve gelatin in boiling water; stir in cold water. With a meat fork or wooden skewer, poke holes in cake about 2 in. apart. Slowly pour gelatin over cake. Refrigerate for 2-3 hours.

3 For frosting, in a small bowl, cream butter until fluffy. Beat in confectioners' sugar, cocoa, milk and vanilla until smooth. Spread over the cake; top with candy pumpkins. Cover and refrigerate until serving.

YIELD: 12-15 SERVINGS.

pumpkin ice cream pie

PREP: 15 MIN. + FREEZING

1 quart vanilla ice cream, softened
3/4 cup canned pumpkin
1/4 cup honey
1/2 teaspoon ground cinnamon
1/4 teaspoon salt
1/4 teaspoon ground ginger
Dash ground nutmeg
Dash ground cloves
1 graham cracker crust (9 inches)
Whipped topping and pecan halves, optional

1 In a large bowl, combine the first eight ingredients; beat until smooth. Spoon into crust. Cover and freeze for 2 hours or until firm.

2 Remove from the freezer 15 minutes before serving. Garnish with whipped topping and pecans if desired.

YIELD: 6-8 SERVINGS.

The holidays are the perfect time to try this quick twist on a traditional pumpkin pie. I often make it ahead, so it goes from freezer to feast!
Marion Stoll • Dent, MN

turkey biscuit bake

PREP/TOTAL TIME: 30 MIN.

As a college student, I appreciate stick-to-your-ribs foods like this that are also easy on the budget. I often double the recipe to ensure leftovers.

Andy Zinkle • Mt. Pleasant, IA

1 can (10-3/4 ounces) condensed cream of chicken soup, undiluted
1 cup diced cooked turkey or chicken
1 can (4 ounces) mushroom stems and pieces, drained
1/2 cup frozen peas
1/4 cup milk
Dash each ground cumin, dried basil and thyme
1 tube (12 ounces) refrigerated biscuits

1 In a large bowl, combine the soup, turkey, mushrooms, peas, milk, cumin, basil and thyme. Pour into a greased 8-in. square baking dish. Arrange biscuits over the top.

2 Bake, uncovered, at 350° for 20-25 minutes or until biscuits are golden brown.

YIELD: 5 SERVINGS.

This simple but special deep-dish pie provides a down-home finish to hearty autumn meals served at home. Pecans and pumpkin-pie spices make this a comforting seasonal classic.

Paul Azzone
Shoreham, NY

sweet potato pie

PREP: 25 MIN. • BAKE: 45 MIN. + COOLING

1-2/3 cups pie crust mix
1/4 cup chopped pecans
3 to 4 tablespoons cold water
3 eggs
2 cans (15 ounces each) sweet potatoes, drained
1 can (14 ounces) sweetened condensed milk
1-1/2 to 2 teaspoons pumpkin pie spice
1 teaspoon vanilla extract
1/2 teaspoon salt
Whipped topping and additional chopped pecans, toasted, optional

1 In a small bowl, combine pie crust mix and pecans. Gradually add water, tossing with a fork until dough forms a ball. Roll out to fit a 9-in. deep-dish pie plate. Transfer pastry to pie plate. Flute edges; set aside.

2 In a food processor, combine the eggs, sweet potatoes, milk, pumpkin pie spice, vanilla and salt; blend until smooth. Pour into pastry.

3 Bake at 425° for 15 minutes. Reduce heat to 350°; bake 30-35 minutes longer or until a knife inserted near the center comes out clean. Cool on a wire rack. Garnish with whipped topping and toasted pecans if desired.

YIELD: 8 SERVINGS.

apricot pumpkin cake

PREP: 5 MIN. • BAKE: 25 MIN. + COOLING

1 cup chopped dried apricots

1 package (14 ounces) pumpkin quick bread/muffin mix

1 cup water

2 eggs

3 tablespoons canola oil

1 can (15 ounces) apricot halves, drained

1 can (16 ounces) cream cheese frosting

1/2 cup chopped pecans

1 Set aside 1/2 cup dried apricots for garnish. In a small bowl, soak the remaining apricots in hot water for 5 minutes; drain well. Puree in a food processor or blender.

2 In a large bowl, combine the quick bread mix, water, eggs, oil and pureed apricots. Stir in canned apricots. Pour into a greased 11-in. x 7-in. baking dish.

3 Bake at 375° for 22-27 minutes or until a toothpick inserted near the center comes out clean. Cool on a wire rack. Frost cake with cream cheese frosting; sprinkle with pecans and reserved apricots. Refrigerate leftovers.

YIELD: 9 SERVINGS.

pretzel-topped sweet potatoes

PREP: 20 MIN. • BAKE: 25 MIN.

2 cups chopped pretzel rods (about 13)
1 cup chopped pecans
1 cup fresh or frozen cranberries
1 cup packed brown sugar
1 cup butter, melted, divided
1 can (2-1/2 pounds) sweet potatoes, drained
1 can (5 ounces) evaporated milk
1/2 cup sugar
1 teaspoon vanilla extract

1 In a large bowl, combine the pretzels, pecans, cranberries, brown sugar and 1/2 cup butter; set aside.

2 In a large bowl, beat the sweet potatoes until smooth. Add the milk, sugar, vanilla and remaining butter; beat until well blended.

3 Spoon into a greased shallow 2-qt. baking dish; sprinkle with pretzel mixture. Bake, uncovered, at 350° for 25-30 minutes or until the edges are bubbly.

YIELD: 10-12 SERVINGS.

Everyone with whom I've shared this recipe says it's the tastiest way to serve sweet potatoes. I like to make it for special dinners and even for brunch as a colorful go-with dish. The mingled sweet, tart and salty flavors are an unusual treat.

Sue Mallory • Lancaster, PA

cran-raspberry pie

PREP: 20 MIN. + CHILLING

Sweet raspberry gelatin tames the tartness of cranberries and pineapple in this holiday pie. The fluffy marshmallow-flavored topping is simply amazing! Plan on having seconds.

Eddie Stott • Mt. Juliet, TN

1 package (3 ounces) raspberry gelatin
1 cup boiling water
1 cup whole-berry cranberry sauce
1 can (8 ounces) unsweetened crushed pineapple, drained
1 graham cracker crust (9 inches)
2 cups miniature marshmallows
1/4 cup sweetened condensed milk
1/2 teaspoon vanilla extract
1 cup heavy whipping cream, whipped

1 In a large bowl, dissolve gelatin in boiling water. Stir in cranberry sauce and pineapple. Chill until partially set. Pour into crust. Refrigerate until set.

2 Meanwhile, in a heavy saucepan, combine marshmallows and milk. Cook and stir over medium-low heat until marshmallows are melted. Remove from the heat. Stir in vanilla. Transfer to a large bowl. Cover and let stand until cooled to room temperature.

3 Whisk in a third of the whipped cream until smooth (mixture will be stringy at first). Fold in the remaining whipped cream. Spread over gelatin layer. Refrigerate until set.

YIELD: 6-8 SERVINGS.

glazed pork roast

PREP: 25 MIN. • BAKE: 2 HOURS + STANDING

1 bone-in pork loin roast (4 to 5 pounds)
1 can (14 ounces) jellied cranberry sauce
1/2 cup water
1/3 cup packed brown sugar
1/3 cup molasses
1/4 cup cider vinegar
1/4 teaspoon ground cloves
1/4 teaspoon ground cinnamon

1 Line a shallow roasting pan with foil; place roast fat side up on a rack in prepared pan. In a small saucepan, combine the remaining ingredients. Bring to a boil. Reduce heat; simmer, uncovered, for 14-16 minutes or until smooth and slightly thickened. Pour over pork.

2 Bake, uncovered, at 325° for 2 to 2-1/2 hours or until a meat thermometer reads 160°, basting with pan juices every 30 minutes. Let stand for 10 minutes before slicing.

YIELD: 10 SERVINGS.

varied vinegars

Cider vinegar has a fruity flavor and is used in recipes for a faint vinegar taste. White vinegar has a sharp flavor and is used when a strong taste is desired. If a recipe does not specify the vinegar, use one that best fits the dish.

I came up with this dish after combining several different recipes. I wrap up each beef tenderloin, topped with a tasty mushroom mixture, in a sheet of puff pastry. It sounds like a lot of work, but it isn't, and it's so elegant.

Julie Mahoney
St. Edward, NE

tenderloin
in puff pastry

PREP: 20 MIN. + CHILLING • BAKE: 20 MIN.

4 beef tenderloin steaks (1-3/4 inches thick and 5 ounces each)

1 tablespoon canola oil

1/2 pound sliced fresh mushrooms

4 green onions, chopped

1/4 cup butter

1/2 teaspoon salt

1/4 teaspoon pepper

1 frozen puff pastry sheet, thawed

1 egg

1 tablespoon water

1 In a large skillet, brown steaks in oil on both sides. Place a wire rack on a baking sheet. Transfer steaks to wire rack; refrigerate for 1 hour. In the same skillet, saute mushrooms and onions in butter until tender; drain. Stir in the salt and pepper.

2 On a lightly floured surface, roll pastry into a 13-in. square. Cut into four squares. Place one steak in the center of each square; top with mushroom mixture. Combine egg and water; brush over pastry.

3 Bring up corners to center and tuck in edges; press to seal. Place on a parchment paper-lined baking sheet. Cover and refrigerate for 1 hour or overnight.

4 Bake, uncovered, at 400° for 20-25 minutes or until pastry is golden brown and meat reaches desired doneness (for medium-rare, a meat thermometer should read 145°; medium, 160°; well-done, 170°).

YIELD: 4 SERVINGS.

eggnog biscuits

PREP/TOTAL TIME: 20 MIN.

  1 cup plus 1 tablespoon biscuit/baking mix

  1/3 cup eggnog

  1/4 to 1/2 teaspoon ground nutmeg

1 In a small bowl, combine biscuit mix and eggnog just until moistened. Turn on a lightly floured surface; knead 8-10 times. Pat or roll out to 1/2-in. thickness; cut with a floured 2-1/2-in. biscuit cutter.

2 Place 2 in. apart on a greased baking sheet. Sprinkle with nutmeg. Bake at 450° for 8-10 minutes or until lightly browned. Serve warm.

YIELD: 6-8 BISCUITS.

EDITOR'S NOTE: This recipe was tested with commercially prepared eggnog.

Served as an hors d'oeuvre or a light main dish, these stuffed mushrooms are pretty and delicious. Canned crabmeat becomes absolutely elegant.

Jennifer Coduto
Kent, OH

crab cake-stuffed portobellos

PREP/TOTAL TIME: 30 MIN.

6 large portobello mushrooms

3/4 cup finely chopped sweet onion

2 tablespoons olive oil, divided

1 package (8 ounces) cream cheese, softened

1 egg

1/2 cup seasoned bread crumbs

1/2 cup plus 1 teaspoon grated Parmesan cheese, divided

1 teaspoon seafood seasoning

2 cans (6-1/2 ounces each) lump crabmeat, drained

1/4 teaspoon paprika

1 Remove stems from mushrooms (discard or save for another use); set caps aside. In a small skillet, saute onion in 1 tablespoon oil until tender. In a small bowl, combine the cream cheese, egg, bread crumbs, 1/2 cup cheese and seafood seasoning. Gently stir in crab and onion.

2 Spoon 1/2 cup crab mixture into each mushroom cap; drizzle with remaining oil. Sprinkle with paprika and remaining cheese. Place in a greased 15-in. x 10-in. x 1-in. baking pan.

3 Bake, uncovered, at 400° for 15-20 minutes or until mushrooms are tender.

YIELD: 6 SERVINGS.

To make my green beans more festive for the holidays, I add dried cranberries. A touch of sweet honey complements the orange peel and tart cranberries.

Darlene Brenden
Salem, OR

holiday green beans

PREP/TOTAL TIME: 15 MIN.

- 1 package (16 ounces) frozen cut green beans
- 1 teaspoon grated orange peel
- 1/2 cup dried cranberries
- 1/2 cup real bacon bits
- 2 tablespoons honey

1 Cook the green beans according to package directions, adding the orange peel during cooking; drain. Add the cranberries, bacon and honey; toss to combine.

YIELD: 4 SERVINGS.

orange peel

Grating fresh orange peel is a lot easier when you place the orange in the freezer the night before.

snowman sugar cookies

PREP: 30 MIN. • BAKE: 10 MIN. + COOLING

1 tube (18 ounces) refrigerated sugar
  cookie dough
1/2 cup shortening
1/2 cup butter, softened
4 cups confectioners' sugar
1 tablespoon whole milk
1 teaspoon vanilla extract
48 miniature semisweet chocolate chips
24 candy corn candies
1/2 cup Red Hots

1 Cut cookie dough into 1/4-in. slices. Place 2 in. apart on ungreased baking sheets. Bake at 350° for 8-12 minutes or until edges are lightly browned. Cool for 2 minutes before removing to wire racks to cool completely.

2 For frosting, in a small bowl, cream shortening and butter. Gradually beat in confectioners' sugar. Beat in milk and vanilla until smooth. Spread over cookies. Decorate with chocolate chips, candy corn and Red Hots.

YIELD: 2 DOZEN.

rudolph treats

PREP/TOTAL TIME: 15 MIN.

12 miniature pretzels, halved
12 fun-size Almond Joy candy bars
12 miniature marshmallows, halved
Black decorating gel
12 red M&M's miniature baking bits

1 Insert an end from two pretzel halves into each candy bar to form antlers. Gently press the cut side of two marshmallow halves onto each candy bar for eyes; dot with decorating gel.

2 For nose, attach an M&M to the top of each candy with decorating gel. Store in an airtight container.

YIELD: 1 DOZEN.

A rich, chocolaty brownie crust is the perfect partner to refreshing peppermint ice cream. My holiday guests have come to expect this make-ahead dessert.

Carol Gillespie
Chambersburg, PA

brownie-peppermint ice cream pie

PREP: 30 MIN. • BAKE: 35 MIN. + FREEZING

1 package fudge brownie mix
  (8-inch square pan size)

1/2 cup vanilla or white chips

1/2 cup 60% cacao bittersweet chocolate
  baking chips

1/3 cup caramel ice cream topping

1 pint peppermint ice cream, softened

1 cup heavy whipping cream

1/4 cup confectioners' sugar

1/8 teaspoon peppermint extract

1/4 cup crushed peppermint candies

1 Prepare brownie batter according to package directions; stir in vanilla and bittersweet chips. Spread onto the bottom and up the sides of a greased 9-in. pie plate.

2 Bake at 350° for 35-40 minutes or until a toothpick inserted near the center comes out clean. Cool for 5 minutes. Gently press down center of crust if necessary. Cool completely on a wire rack.

3 Drizzle caramel topping over crust; spread evenly with ice cream. Cover and freeze for 4 hours or until firm.

4 Remove from the freezer 10 minutes before serving. Meanwhile, in a small bowl, beat cream, confectioners' sugar and extract until stiff peaks form. Spread over ice cream; sprinkle with the crushed peppermints.

YIELD: 8 SERVINGS.

squash (also see zucchini)

Stuffing Squash Casserole, 58
Tortellini Primavera, 150

strawberries & strawberry jam

Berry-Filled Doughnuts, 43
Chocolate Hazelnut
   Parfaits, 190
Coconut Strawberry Phyllo
   Cones, 201
Star-Spangled Fruit Tart, 223
Star-Spangled Shortcake, 222
Strawberries 'n' Cream
   French Toast Sticks, 40
Strawberry Banana
   Squares, 203
Strawberry Braid, 88

stuffing mix

Apple Stuffing, 57
Cranberry Pear Stuffing, 64
Dried Fruit Stuffing, 69
Rich Mushroom Bake, 64
Smothered Pork Chops, 129
Stuffing-Coated Chicken, 128
Stuffing Squash Casserole, 58
Vegetable Stuffing Bake, 67

sweet potatoes

Pretzel-Topped Sweet
   Potatoes, 233
Sweet Potato Pie, 231

sweet rolls
(also see hot roll mix)

Orange Coffee Cake Ring, 38
Peachy Rolls, 97

tomatoes & sun-dried tomatoes

Bacon-Olive Tomato Pizza, 149
Basil Tomato Soup, 107
Beefy Tomato Rice Skillet, 153
Confetti Cheese Salsa, 16
Herbed Chicken and
   Tomatoes, 175
Mozzarella Tomato Tartlets, 20
Pepperoni Cheese Twists, 15
Tomato Bacon Cups, 17
Tomato Salmon Bake, 146
Tortellini Appetizers, 10
Zesty Salsa, 18

turkey

Brunch Pockets, 45
Ranch Turkey Pasta Dinner, 159
Slow-Cooked Turkey
   Sandwiches, 178
Turkey Biscuit Bake, 230
Turkey Noodle Stew, 109
Turkey with Cranberry
   Sauce, 165
Veggie Turkey Casserole, 139

vegetables: canned, frozen & fresh
(also see specific kinds)

Asian Noodle Toss, 152
Au Gratin Ham Potpie, 151
Beef Macaroni Soup, 105
California Quiche, 44
Cheese Ravioli with
   Veggies, 157
Chicken Cheese Soup, 104
Chicken in Baskets, 152
Chicken Pasta Primavera, 154
Colorful Chicken Pasta, 156
Creamy Italian Spiral
   Salad, 65
Home-Style Stew, 171
Macaroni Vegetable Soup, 106
Mock Chinese Soup, 113
Pasta Meatball Soup, 115
Pepperoni Pasta Salad, 62
Ranch Turkey Pasta
   Dinner, 159
Shrimp 'n' Veggie Pizza, 158
Speedy Vegetable Soup, 111
Vegetable Cheese Soup, 116
Vegetable Stuffing Bake, 67
Veggie Turkey Casserole, 139

waffles

Apple Waffle Grills, 42
Light 'n' Crispy Waffles, 38
Pecan-Stuffed Waffles, 41

whipped topping

Black Forest Cheesecake, 198
Blueberry Fluff Pie, 204
Coconut Strawberry Phyllo
   Cones, 201
Fluffy Chocolate Pie, 185
Grasshopper Pie, 196
Poppy Seed Lemon Pie, 218
Pudding Pound Cake
   Dessert, 208
Vanilla Chip Dessert, 200
Wearing o' Green Cake, 221

yogurt

Orange Crunch Yogurt, 49
Polynesian Parfaits for Two, 39

zucchini (also see squash)

Sweet-and-Sour Zucchini, 54
Tortellini Primavera, 150

COOKING TERMS

Here's a quick reference for some of the cooking terms used in *Taste of Home* recipes:

BASTE—To moisten food with melted butter, pan drippings, marinades or other liquid to add more flavor and juiciness.

BEAT—A rapid movement to combine ingredients using a fork, spoon, wire whisk or electric mixer.

BLEND—To combine ingredients until just mixed.

BOIL—To heat liquids until bubbles form that cannot be "stirred down." In the case of water, the temperature will reach 212°.

BONE—To remove all meat from the bone before cooking.

CREAM—To beat ingredients together to a smooth consistency, usually in the case of butter and sugar for baking.

DASH—A small amount of seasoning, less than 1/8 teaspoon. If using a shaker, a dash would comprise a quick flip of the container.

DREDGE—To coat foods with flour or other dry ingredients. Most often done with pot roasts and stew meat before browning.

FOLD—To incorporate several ingredients by careful and gentle turning with a spatula. Used generally with beaten egg whites or whipped cream when mixing into the rest of the ingredients to keep the batter light.

JULIENNE—To cut foods into long thin strips much like matchsticks. Used most often for salads and stir-fry dishes.

MINCE—To cut into very fine pieces. Used often for garlic or fresh herbs.

PARBOIL—To cook partially, usually used in the case of chicken, sausages and vegetables.

PARTIALLY SET—Describes the consistency of gelatin after it has been chilled for a small amount of time. Mixture should resemble the consistency of egg whites.

PUREE—To process foods to a smooth mixture. Can be prepared in an electric blender, food processor, food mill or sieve.

SAUTE—To fry quickly in a small amount of fat, stirring almost constantly. Most often done with onions, mushrooms and other chopped vegetables.

SCORE—To cut slits partway through the outer surface of foods. Often used with ham or flank steak.

STIR-FRY—To cook meats and/or vegetables with a constant stirring motion in a small amount of oil in a wok or skillet over high heat.